WebPlus X2
Resource Guide

How to contact us

Contacting Serif technical support

Our support mission is to provide fast, friendly technical advice and support from a team of on-call experts. Technical support is provided from our Web support page, and useful information can be obtained via our web-based forums (see below). There are no pricing policies after the 30 day money back guarantee period.

UK/International/ US Technical Support :	**http://www.serif.com/support**

Additional Serif contact information

Web:

Serif Web Site:	**http://www.serif.com**
Forums:	**http://www.serif.com/forums.asp**

Main office (UK, Europe):

The Software Centre, PO Box 2000, Nottingham, NG11 7GW, UK

Main:	(0115) 914 2000
Registration (UK only):	(0800) 376 1989
Sales (UK only):	(0800) 376 7070
Customer Service (UK/International):	**http://www.serif.com/support**
General Fax:	(0115) 914 2020

North American office (US, Canada):

The Software Center, 13 Columbia Drive, Suite 5, Amherst NH 03031, USA

Main:	(603) 889-8650
Registration:	(800) 794-6876
Sales:	(800) 55-SERIF or 557-3743
Customer Service:	**http://www.serif.com/support**
General Fax:	(603) 889-1127

International enquiries

Please contact our main office.

Contents

Chapter 4 - Colour Schemes..375

Introduction

Welcome to the WebPlus X2 Resource Guide! Whether you are new to WebPlus X2 or a seasoned Web publisher, the *Resource Guide* offers content to help you get the best out of WebPlus. From a range of novice and professional tutorials to get you started or help you accomplish a complex project, to full-colour previews of the Design Templates, Theme Graphics and Colour Schemes, the *Resource Guide* is something you'll return to time and time again.

About the Resource Guide

The *Resource Guide* is your key to getting even more out of WebPlus and is organized into the following chapters:

- **Tutorials**—Illustrated, step-by-step training covering the basics of WebPlus and Web site design, along with some more challenging projects.

- **Web Site & Email Templates**—A useful gallery showing the various Web Site and Email Design Templates available with WebPlus X2 and its Resource CD.

- **Theme Graphics**—Full colour previews of the Theme Graphic sets available with WebPlus.

- **Colour Schemes**—Attractive previews of the WebPlus X2 Colour Schemes.

How the Resource Guide was made

This full-colour *Resource Guide* was created and output using PagePlus, and employing many PagePlus features. These features include:

- BookPlus to unify separate publications with a common page numbering system.

- Mail and Photo Merge with Repeating Areas to automatically create pages with picture content based on a folder of images.

- Find and Replace functionality to apply text styles consistently and quickly throughout the text.

Finally, the content was incorporated into a PagePlus Book comprised of multiple publication 'chapters.' The book was then published as a press-ready PDF—accurately maintaining all text, fonts, images, and native colouring—in a CMYK colour format suitable for professional printing.

Tutorials

Welcome to the WebPlus X2 tutorials.

These exercises provide step-by-step instructions to help you get the most out of WebPlus, and guide you through the process of creating professional-looking and effective Web sites. The tutorials are grouped into the following categories:

Getting Started

Aimed at the new user, these exercises introduce you to the WebPlus user interface, and the key tools and features required to create a Web site. The step-by-step approach will develop your understanding of Web site creation and guide you to explore the program's possibilities.

Creating Personal Web Sites

The emphasis here is on combining various approaches to achieve impressive results, and tackling some of the more common personal Web site design scenarios.

Creating Business Web Sites

In these tutorials, the focus is on creating and enhancing business Web sites. However, many of the techniques and features illustrated can be used just as effectively on a personal Web site.

If you're looking for a tutorial to address your specific needs or interests, see the list on the following page.

The tutorials are presented as PDF files, which you can print out or view onscreen.

If viewing onscreen, you can quickly switch between WebPlus and the tutorial document by pressing the **Alt + Tab** keys.

For information on: **See...**

Planning & preparing

Domain names, Web host providers   *Setting up a Commercial Site (NEW)*

Accessing free Web space   *Accessing Your Free Web Space*

Colour

Creating & choosing colours   *Working With Colour Schemes*

E-Commerce

Adding e-commerce functionality   *Creating an E-Commerce Web Site*

Choosing a shopping cart provider

Popup rollovers

Creating popup rollovers   *Creating a Personal Web Site*

Database merge   *Creating an Image Catalogue (NEW)*

Navigation & design elements

Using theme graphics & templates;   *Using Theme Graphics & the WebPlus*
adding gallery elements   *Gallery; Building a Web Site*

Inserting Flash™ banners   *Adding Flash Objects to Your Site*

Photo galleries

Creating photo galleries   *Creating a Personal Web Site*

     Adding a Flash Photo Gallery (NEW)

Serif Web Resources

Accessing Serif Web Resources   *Adding Dynamic Content to Your Site*

Site accessibility & ease-of-use

Image resolution & resizing   *Importing Images; Creating Web-Friendly*
     Sites; Optimizing Your Site for Search
Search engine optimization   *Engines*

Smart objects

Creating hit counters, blogs, shout   *Adding Dynamic Content to Your Site*
boxes, mailing lists, & polls.

Adding forums   *Adding a Forum (NEW)*

Web-based forms

Creating forms & form controls   *Creating a Personal Web Site*

Publishing & maintenance

Publishing & maintaining Web sites   *Previewing & Publishing Your Web Site*

Getting Started

Combining hands-on examples with some essential theory, the Getting Started sequence offers an introduction to Web page design in general, and the WebPlus environment in particular.

- Introducing WebPlus X2
- Working With Text
- Creating Hyperlinks
- Importing Images
- Using Theme Graphics and the Gallery
- Previewing and Publishing
- Accessing Your Free Web Space
- Introducing HTML
- Building a Web Site
- Working With Colour Schemes
- Creating Web-Friendly Sites

Using other WebPlus resources

The tutorials and projects give you the opportunity to gain hands-on experience with basic WebPlus tools, and cover the concepts and features required to complete the exercises. For more information on specific features and topics, see the WebPlus online Help and the **How To** tab.

To access online Help:

1   Click **Help**, then **WebPlus Help** (or press **F1**).

    The **Help** window initially displays its **Contents** pane on the left, and the **Visual Reference** menu on the right.

2   Click the book icons in the **Contents** list to expand them; click a document icon to display a topic.

    - or -

    Click directly on Visual Reference graphics to browse interface features like menus and toolbars.

    - or -

    Click the **Index** tab to browse the list of key terms.

    - or -

    Click the **Search** tab to look up specific terms using full-text search.

Introducing WebPlus X2

Serif

WEBPLUS X2
Website Maker

What do you want to do?

Create
- Start New Site
- Use Design Template

Open
- Open Saved Site
- Import Existing Site

View
- Sample Websites
- Browse Tutorials

Don't show this wizard again   Choose Workspace <Current Profile>

WebPlus provides simple, powerful tools that make it easy to
design clearly structured Web sites that are easy to navigate.
In this tutorial, we'll use a WebPlus template to introduce
you to the basic elements of site structure. You'll familiarize
yourself with the WebPlus workspace, and learn how to:

- Open a WebPlus template site.
- Make adjustments to and preview a site.
- View site structure.
- Add and rearrange pages.

Getting Started

WebPlus lets you assemble all the elements of your site-in-progress into one multi-page document that is saved as a WebPlus project file.

You can then publish the project as a set of pages that comprise your Web site. WebPlus takes the pages and converts them to HTML.

> A Web site is basically a collection of separate pages with hyperlinks connecting them. Any visitor who enters your site will need help getting around. As the 'architect' of this entity, it's your job to arrange your content in a logical and accessible way, and provide navigational signposts that quickly convey how the site is organized.

Creating a Web site in WebPlus can be as simple as choosing and customizing a design template—or you can start from scratch. Templates simplify things by providing you with a variety of professionally designed starter layouts. We'll start by using a Web site template, which you can customize to suit your needs.

1 Open WebPlus, or if WebPlus is already running, choose **File**, then **Startup Wizard**.

2 The Startup Wizard provides the following options:

- **Create > Start New Site**—to create a new project from scratch, starting with a blank Home page.

- **Create > Use Design Template**—to use a predesigned template as a starting point for your project.

- **Open > Open Saved Site**—to edit existing WebPlus project files.

- **Open > Import Existing Site**—to convert existing HTML resources.

- **View > Sample Websites**—to see professionally designed examples.

    View > Browse Tutorials—to view the list of tutorials.

3 Click **Create > Use Design Template**.

4 In the **New Site** dialog, in the left templates list, scroll down to the **Interest** category and select the template, **Reactive**.

Zoom into the template for a better view.

In the right **Pages** pane, you can choose which pages to add to your site by selecting or clearing the option boxes. For now, leave the default setting (all selected).

At the top of the dialog, you can also choose a **Button Theme** for the site and the colour **Scheme**. Leave these at the default settings for now and click **Open**.

The template site opens with the **Home** page displayed in the workspace. This is a simple site with just eight pages; at the right of the workspace you'll see them listed on the **Site** tab.

5 On the toolbar at the top of the workspace, click the arrow on the **HTML Preview** button to expand a list of preview options.

6 Select **Preview Site in <your Web browser of choice>**. WebPlus generates the necessary temporary files and opens a new browser window displaying the site's Home page.

7 At the top of the page you'll see a **navigation bar** (navbar) consisting of five buttons. Click the buttons to navigate quickly between the five 'top-level' pages of the site.

The navbar interconnects the site's pages and is an indispensable element of site design. Users will expect it to be there, they'll know what to do with it, and it will help them grasp your site's main content sections at a glance.

> 💡 The **WebPlus Theme Graphics** tab includes a selection of predesigned navigation bars that you can add to your site with a single drag-and-drop operation!
>
> See the "Getting Started: Using Theme Graphics and the Gallery" tutorial.

Once you've experimented with the navbar, close the browser window and return to WebPlus.

8 Before proceeding, click **File**, then **Save**, and save your project file with a file name of your choice. Note that saving the WebPlus (.wpp) project file is not the same as publishing it as a Web site.

Let's take a few moments to examine the site we created from the template.

The WebPlus workspace consists of:

- A **page area**, where you put the text, graphics, and other elements you want to appear on the final Web page.

- A surrounding **pasteboard area**, where you can keep elements that are being prepared or waiting to be positioned on the page area.

- Horizontal and vertical **toolbars** and **tabs**, used to access WebPlus commands and tools.

Move the mouse pointer around the screen and you'll see popup **tooltips** that identify toolbar buttons and flyouts.

Right-click any object or page region to bring up a **context menu** of functions... the choices probably seem overwhelming at this point!

> 💡 The **Hintline** toolbar at the bottom of the workspace provides context-sensitive information and tips about selected objects, buttons, and menu items.

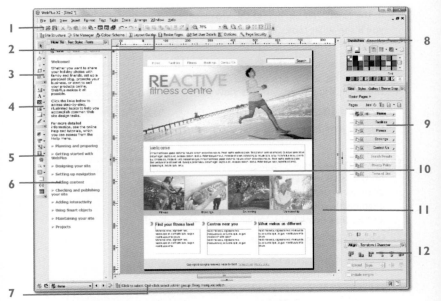

1 Standard, Arrange and View toolbars

2 Context toolbars

3 Tools toolbar

4 Standard Objects toolbar

5 Web Objects toolbar

6 How To, Text Styles, & Fonts tabs

7 Hintline toolbar

8 Swatches, Colour, Line, Transparency tabs

9 Site, Style, Gallery, Theme Graphics tabs

10 Page area

11 Pasteboard area

12 Align, Transform, Character tabs

Let's now look at some different ways to get an overview of the entire site.

9 At the right of the workspace, click the **Site** tab. This tab displays the **Site Structure tree** for this particular site. You'll recognize the entries as the main pages of the site.

10 Double-click a page entry to open it in the workspace.

As you change pages, notice that the ⊕ Displayed Page icon moves to indicate which page is currently in view and ready for editing.

11 In the lower left corner of the workspace, you'll see what looks like a text field showing the name of the current page.

12 Click the arrow on this **Page Locator** to display a list of the site's pages. This time, single-click any page entry to view it.

Watch the **Site** tab and you'll see the  icon indicating the page on view.

When the Page Locator is selected, you can press your keyboard arrow keys to step between pages.

13 Now try single-clicking page entries on the **Site** tab. This time nothing changes in the workspace, but each page entry you click changes colour and its title turns bold. What does change, then?

When using the Site tab list:

- Single-click a page to *select* it— which you might do, for example, if you wanted to delete the page, or change its properties.

The vertical order of the Web pages corresponds to the order in which they appear in the navbar. Page entries are connected by dotted lines, implying a certain relatedness.

- Double-click a page to *view* it or edit its design elements.

This distinction between single- and double-clicking allows you to set the properties of any page, regardless of which page you're editing in the workspace. We'll explore this later.

14 On the context toolbar click ▤ Site Structure .

This dialog provides yet another overview of the pages in the site, plus a variety of other functions.

Click **Close**.

Let's head back to the Studio's **Site** tab to further explore the concept of site structure.

15 On the **Site** tab, right-click the entry for the **Contact Us** page, and choose **Insert Page**.

16 In the **Insert Page** dialog:

- In the **Properties** section, in the **Page name** text box, type 'Joe'.

- In the **Placement** section, select **Child of**.

- Leave all other settings and click **OK**.

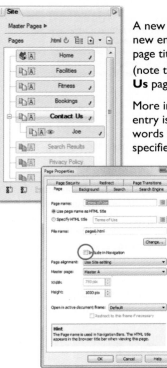

A new page opens in the workspace, along with a new entry on the **Site** tab— which tells us the page title is 'Joe' and that it's currently on view (note the icon) but not selected (the **Contact Us** page still has that honour).

More importantly, notice that the new 'Joe' page entry is indented under **Contact Us**—in other words it's a *child* of **Contact Us**, just as we specified in the dialog.

17 Note also that the pages at the bottom of the list are a different colour and do not have a red check mark next to their names. This is because these pages are not included in the site navigation and therefore do not display on the navbar.

To prove our point, right-click one of the pages and choose **Page Properties**; you'll see that the **Include in Navigation** check box is not selected.

18 In the Site Structure tree, click to select the entry for the **Fitness** page and drag it up into the group of pages at the 'top' level (above **Facilities**).

Notice that the navbar has updated automatically, mirroring the new top-level page order.

Home	Fitness	Facilities	Bookings	Contact Us

19 Click on the **Fitness** page again and this time drag it back down below the **Facilities** entry, restoring its original position.

Check the navbar again and you'll see it has also reverted.

20 Take a few moments to play with moving pages around in the tree. Watch the cursor change when you drag:

🔋 Web page hierarchy

Having inserted a new page in the 'Contact Us' section of the site, we now have the makings of a hierarchy. Now the dotted lines connecting the page entries make more sense, and the Site Structure tree is no longer just a list.

You can see how this parent-and-child 'tree' structure provides a natural framework for organizing site content into sections and levels. In this site, we've begun with one main page at the top level for each of our main sections: Home, Fitness, Facilities, Bookings and Contact Us. Over time we would expect to add subsidiary (child) pages to each section, at lower levels.

- indicates that you can make the dropped page a child of the page above.

- indicates that the page will land on the same level.

The buttons at the bottom of the **Site** tab also allow you to quickly and easily change pages from child to parent, or to move pages up or down in the list. To use any of these buttons, select the page that you want to move and then click the relevant button.

If you move a parent page, notice that its child pages go with it—since they are dependent on it.

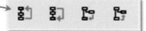

You can also rearrange pages in the **Site Structure** dialog (accessed via the **File** menu) by dragging and dropping in a similar way to the site tab. The cursors are slightly different:

- ⌐ indicates that the page will stay on the same level

- ⌐ indicates that the page will become a child of the page above.

Select the **Facilities** page, then right-click and select **Page Properties**.

In the **Page Properties** dialog, clear the **Include in Navigation** check box and then click **OK**.

Notice what happens in the navbar: Switching off the **Include in Navigation** setting for a page forces navbars to ignore that page, and its button disappears.

23 Click on another page on the **Site** tab.

Now take a look at the **page list**. Notice that the **Facilities** entry has changed colour and its red check mark is no longer displayed.

24 Open the **Page Properties** dialog again and select the **Include in Navigation** check box to reset it.

Because most people grasp a branching structure fairly quickly, organizing your content into a 'tree' structure helps your visitor navigate through it. As we've seen in this tutorial, the WebPlus Site Structure tree serves as a control centre that lets you, the designer, not only visualize your site's framework but manipulate it with ease.

You now understand a little about site structure and how theme graphic navigation bars adapt instantly to changes in the structure. At this point, you can either proceed to the next tutorial for an introduction to text objects, or, for more hands-on experience with theme graphics, you can go directly to "Getting Started: Using Theme Graphics and the Gallery" and begin working with these amazing objects!

Working With Text

Lorem ipsum dolor...

Text and images form the foundation of information delivery via the Internet. In particular, HTML text is extremely fast to deliver to viewers' screens.

In this exercise, we'll discuss the details surrounding the creation and editing of text.

- Create and edit Artistic, Creative, and HTML text frames.
- Learn about text flow, text resizing, and the Text Manager.
- Edit text in WritePlus.

Working With Text

1   From the WebPlus Startup Wizard, choose **Create > Start New Site** (or from the **File** menu, choose **New**).

Note that there are two text tool buttons on the left toolbar:

- The **Text** flyout provides a selection of tools for creating artistic text and various kinds of text-on-a-path (see "Putting text on a path" in online Help).

- The **Text Frame** flyout allows you to create 🖼 **HTML** or 🖼 **Creative** text frames. HTML frames are useful for Web 'optimization' purposes. We'll explain this later.

2   Click the Ａ **Artistic Text** tool and then drag the mouse cursor until the text size is approximately 100 points—as you drag, watch the Hintline to see the text size. Release the mouse button and type a word.

Once you have created your text object, WebPlus reverts to the ▶ **Pointer** tool.

💡 To redock a tab or toolbar, double-click its header.

3   Click the grey border of the text object to select it. Now any changes you make to your object will apply to all of its contents. Let's start by choosing a colour for our text.

4   Click the **Swatches** tab and then click its header and drag it out of the Studio to 'undock' it. Increase the size of the tab by clicking and dragging a corner.

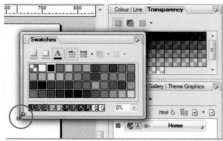

5   Click to expand the **Palettes** drop-down list. Select a palette, and then click a colour swatch to apply it to the text.

6 Move your cursor over the text, click inside the text object and type a letter. As you approach, move over, and then move inside the object's bounding box, note the change from Pointer cursor to Move cursor to I-beam text editing cursor.

Let's now create some **Creative** and **HTML** text frames.

7 On the Text Frame flyout, select the 🄰 **Creative Frame** tool and click once on the page to insert a standard-size text frame. Type until your frame is overflowing with text.

(To fill the frame with placeholder text, click **Insert>Fill with Placeholder Text**. Reduce the frame size so that the text overflows.)

Artistic

💡 Use the **Swatches** tab to apply preset solid colours, gradient fills, bitmap fills, and shading. WebPlus provides a selection of galleries and palettes from which to choose. You can also add your own colours and fills (for more information see online Help).

Curabitur felis erat, tempus eu, placerat et, pellentesque sed, purus. Sed sed diam. Nam nunc. Class aptent taciti sociosqu ad litora torquent per conubia nostra, per inceptos hymenaeos. Aenean risus est, porttitor vel, placerat sit amet, vestibulum sit

npus eu, e sed, purus. ic. Class aptent a torquent per eptos us est, pc estibulu

amet, nibh. Ut faucibus justo quis nisl. Etiam vulputate, sapien eu egestas rutrum, leo neque luctus dolor, sed hendrerit tortor metus ut dui. Etiam id pede porttitor turpis tristique lacinia.

8 Create a second Creative text frame, but this time click and drag on the page to set the size of your frame.

9 Click the ▭ **Link** button at the bottom of your first text frame. The cursor changes to a jug.

10 Move the cursor over your new text frame and note that the cursor changes to a pouring jug.

11 Click inside the new frame and your text will flow into it. The **Link** button changes to ▬ to show that there is no overflowing text in the second frame.

Typing in the first frame now displaces text into the second frame. The first frame will now display a [⏷] **Link** button, showing that the story is continued in another frame. The link between will remain unless you break it (using [⬚] **Unlink** on the Frame context toolbar).

12 Click the Text Frame flyout again. This time select the [⊞] ▾ **HTML Frame** tool and click once on your page to insert a standard-size text frame. Type until your frame is overflowing with text.

13 Hover over the [⬚] **Link** button at the bottom of the text frame. WebPlus warns you that this is an HTML text frame, which cannot be linked to other frames.

> This is an HTML text frame which cannot be linked to another frame.

When working with HTML frames, you'll need to keep this in mind and ensure that all of your frames are sized appropriately to fit the text you want to display inside them.

Later in the tutorial, we'll explain why you might want to use HTML text frames in your Web site.

14 Select the HTML text frame, then on the Text context bar click the arrow to expand the font list. You can choose any font for your HTML text. For best possible results, we recommend that you select from the Websafe fonts, which are provided at the top of the list and denoted with a checkmark.

For more information, see online Help.

We've introduced you to the three different kinds of text objects provided in WebPlus. Now that you know how to create them, let's continue experimenting and find out why and when you might choose one over the other.

Artistic text

Artistic text is especially useful for headlines, pull quotes, and other special-purpose text. It is easily formatted with the standard text tools, but has some artistic advantages over frame text. For example, you can initially 'draw' artistic text at a desired point size (as you did in the previous section), and drag it to adjust the size later.

In WebPlus, text objects and Creative text frames can take different line styles, fills (including gradient and bitmap fills), and transparency for stunning pictorial effects. You can even flip artistic text and it will remain editable! Let's try a few examples.

1 Click and drag the handles at the edges of your artistic text object and manipulate them.

Note that the text inside stretches with the object itself.

If that stretching is just in the vertical or horizontal dimension the object will be published as a *graphic*, rather than as text.

2 As a comparison, try resizing the Creative and HTML text frames.

Notice how this just resizes the *container* for the text, not the text itself—which stays the same size unless you reformat it.

Lorem ipsum dolor sit amet, consectetuer adipiscing elit. Cras gravida sem ut massa. Quisque accumsan porttitor dui. Sed interdum, nisl ut consequat tristique, lacus nulla porta massa, sed imperdiet sem nunc vitae eros.

Lorem ipsum dolor sit amet, consectetuer adipiscing elit. Cras gravida sem ut massa. Quisque accumsan porttitor dui. Sed interdum, nisl ut consequat tristique, lacus nulla porta massa, sed imperdiet sem nunc vitae eros.

3 Select the artistic text object again, ensuring that you select the surrounding box and not just the text, and then click the **Styles** tab.

4 In the category list at the top of the tab, click on the '+' symbol to expand the **Object Styles**, then repeat to expand **Materials**.

Select the **Wood** category, and then click the swatch of your choice to apply it to your text object.

The **Styles** tab provides a collection of effects that you can apply to objects on your Web site. Click through the various categories and experiment to see the different effects you can achieve.

When you publish your Web site, any text that uses a non-solid fill, a line style other than **None**, a filter effect, a 3D effect, transparency, or horizontal or vertical resizing will be output as a **graphic** (which makes your pages load more slowly compared to using plain text). Artistic text that does not have these effects applied will be output as **text**.

For more information, see the "Getting Started: Creating Web-Friendly Sites" tutorial.

Creative frame text

Creative text frames are useful when you want your text to 'flow' through a series of frames, for example, to shape large areas of text around images.

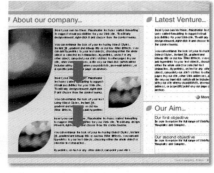

Note, however, that because Web-publishing standards do not support columns or linked frames in the same way as WebPlus, you may notice some difference in designed and published text justification.

WebPlus includes a built-in 'story editor' (WritePlus), which makes it easier for you to view and edit the full text of an entire story that may be spread over many frames or pages—much more convenient than editing text on the page. (And for other tasks, such as exporting story text, it's essential—for details, see online Help.) Let's take a look at the WritePlus environment.

1   To launch WritePlus, select one of your linked Creative text frame objects, then from the **Edit** menu, click **Edit Story** (or click 🔠). WritePlus offers full access to all of WebPlus's text handling features in a handy word processor interface. There's a choice of seeing text in draft or formatted mode, at varied zoom levels, and more.

You can import and export text files, apply paragraph and character styles, and use the spell checker and proof reading tools alongside additional functions such as a word count.

Text you type in WritePlus appears simultaneously in the main WebPlus workspace—because you are working with the same text object.

However, in WritePlus you are simply seeing an alternative view; a view more like a word processor than a Web (or desktop) publisher. Some people prefer editing text objects in WritePlus, others prefer editing in-place, on the page, in WebPlus. There's no right or wrong way, and each method has its merits.

> 💡 You can also use WritePlus to edit HTML frame text and artistic text, but it's particularly useful for editing Creative text that flows between a series of linked frames.

2 When you've finished editing objects in WritePlus, click ✓ **Finish** (or the standard **Close** button in the upper right corner of the WritePlus workspace) to return to WebPlus.

HTML frame text

Any time you add effects such as bitmap fills, transparency, and filter effects to an artistic text object, the object is converted to a graphic when it is published.

Similarly, in a Creative text frame, if you use an unusual font that your site visitors do not have installed, the text will instead be rendered as a graphic. In each of these cases, the end result is the same: an increase in the time it takes your site visitors to download the content of your Web site. If it's important to minimize the amount of time it takes site visitors to access the information on your Web site, you should use HTML text frames.

> 💡 You can choose any font you like for your HTML text.
>
> However, unless you are certain that your site visitors have a particular 'non-Websafe' font installed on their computers, we recommend that you select from the Websafe list for best possible results.
>
> Although 'non-Websafe' text will not be converted to a graphic, you have no way of knowing how it will appear onscreen to site visitors.

The following list outlines the main advantages of using HTML frames.

*   The text contained in HTML frames is always published as text and is never converted to a graphic.

*   HTML frames are searchable by Web search engines such as Google™.

*   HTML frames offer you the ability to design with HTML-compliant styles, which means that you can format text in your HTML frame using heading styles from HI, H2, ..., to H6.

An advantage of this is that text applied with <Hn> styles are given priority over <P> styles (the default) in Internet search engines, with the <HI> tag being given highest priority.

To apply an HTML meta tag

1   Select the HTML frame to change all of the text or select only the relevant paragraph.

2   Click or hover over the ⊳ handle (near the Web Objects toolbar) to open the **Text Styles** tab.

3   Select **Show All** to see all of the text style options.

4   Click on "Heading1" to apply the HI tag, "Heading 2" for the H2 tag and so on. In most cases, you'll probably want to use a combination of text objects—for example, artistic text for titles and HTML or Creative text frames for your main content.

For more information on creating and publishing text and text frames, see "Understanding text frames" in online Help, or the "Getting Started: Creating Web-Friendly Sites" tutorial.

Text Styles	▷
Heading 1	¶
Heading 2	¶
Heading 3	¶
Heading 4	¶
Heading 5	¶
Heading 6	¶

☑ Preview Styles ☑ Show All
🎨 Manage Styles 🔍 Create Style

The **Text Styles** tab contains preset Heading styles which translate to HTML tags HI to H6. You can format the text style to suit your site design whilst keeping those important tags. For more information on modifying text styles see online Help.

Text Manager

Before we end this tour of text objects and move on to our next topic, let's take a quick look at a very useful tool—the **Text Manager**.

1   On the **Tools** menu, select **Site Manager > Text Manager...**

The **Site Manager** dialog shows what text objects you have in your site. You can resize this dialog box to display all of the text options.

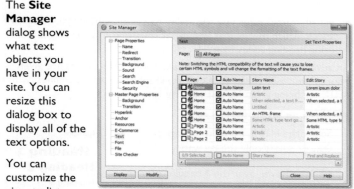

You can customize the view to list page by page or all pages.

For each text object, the following information is provided:

- Page
- Story Name (i.e. Title) - these are auto-generated but you can change them.
- Edit Story (i.e. Contents)
- Font Type
- Font Size
- Paragraph Style
- HTML Compatibility

2   To jump to a specific text object, select it and click **Display**.

3   To return to WebPlus, click **Close**.

We've covered many useful tips for creating, editing, and managing text with WebPlus. We hope that you're now feeling more comfortable with the different text objects we've described and are ready to get started creating content for your own site!

Creating Hyperlinks

WebPlus provides a wide and very flexible range of hyperlink options. This means easy navigation for your site's visitors—and possibly a more efficient visit if your site includes large pictures.

In this exercise, you'll learn how to:

- Create text objects and import pictures.
- Create anchors.
- Create and edit hyperlinks.
- Create self-linking picture hyperlinks.

Creating Hyperlinks

In this tutorial, we'll explore the various hyperlink options and demonstrate a couple of useful WebPlus features.

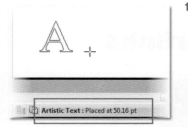

Artistic Text : Placed at 50.16 pt

1 From the Startup Wizard, choose **Create > Start New Site** (or click **File**, and then click **New**).

Our project has one page and no content—we'll add some content to demonstrate the use of hyperlinks, but we won't build a full site.

2 Select the A **Artistic Text** tool and drag the mouse cursor until the text size is approximately 50 points—as you drag, watch the Hintline to see the text size.

3 Write a title for your page and place the text near the upper-middle section of your page.

4 We're about to work with some smaller text objects, so you may want to zoom in a little now. Create a mid-size text object to the left of the page (we've used a 24 pt text size) and type 'Section 1.'

5. Hold down the **Ctrl** key, then click and drag the text object down a little. Release the mouse button to drop a copy of the text object on your page.

6 Repeat the previous step twice to create a total of four text objects. Edit the text objects so that they read Section 1, Section 2, Section 3, and Section 4.

7 Click on a blank area of the page so you have no objects selected. Now click and drag your mouse diagonally across the objects and release the mouse button when the rectangular selection box encompasses them all.

Right-click the group and click **Arrange**, then click **Align Objects**.

8 In the **Align Objects** dialog:

- In the **Distribute** section, choose **Space evenly down** (vertical).

- In the **Horizontally** section, choose **Left**.

- Click **OK**.

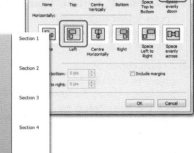

9 Select the **Section 1** text object. On the Tools toolbar, click to expand the ▧ ▾ **Hyperlink** flyout and then click the ⚓ **Anchor** button (or right-click the object and select **Anchor**).

In the **Anchor** dialog box, type 'Section1,' and then click **OK**. (Note that anchor names cannot contain spaces.)

We've just added an 'anchor' to one of our objects. But what does it do? Simply put, it's like placing a bookmark in a book; it defines a place you can jump to quickly.

However, an anchor doesn't just take you to a certain page like a bookmark does, it allows a hyperlink to take you to a specific point on a Web page!

10 Repeat the previous step for each of your text objects, naming the anchors to correspond with the section names.

Anchor

Name of the anchor:

Section1

☐ Include Anchor In Navigation

Title of the anchor:

OK   Cancel

🔍 Anchors can be added to any object on any page, so it's possible to create unique navigation, and to offer speedy access to your site's content.

Anchors for important parts of you site can be included within site navigation maps or navbars by checking the **Include Anchor In Navigation** option. (Make sure that you give the anchor a meaningful title as this is what your site visitors will see.)

Before making our hyperlinks, we need to create objects to hyperlink to...

11 Select the A **Artistic Text** tool and click once on the page to create a text object with default settings. Type 'Section 1' again.

12 Create copies of the object as described previously (steps 5 and 6). Edit the text objects to match the section headers created earlier.

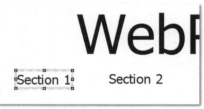

13 Position the text objects in a row under your title text and then select them all by dragging a selection bounding box around them.

On the **Align** tab, click ▪ **Centre Vertically** and ▪ **Space Evenly Across**.

14 Click on the **Section 1** text object near the top of your page to select it.

Click on the grey border of the object to select it as a whole—if there is a flashing 'text-edit' cursor then your hyperlink will not link from the entire line of text.

15 Click the arrow next to the ⚓ **Anchor** tool to display the Hyperlink flyout again, then click the 🔗 **Hyperlink** tool.

16 In the **Hyperlinks** dialog:

- Select **Anchor**.

- All of your site's anchors are listed in the **Anchors** drop-down list. Choose the anchor called **Section1**.

- In the **Title** text box, type 'Click to go to Section 1.'

- Click **OK**.

17 Repeat the previous step to add hyperlinks between the remaining small text objects and section heading anchors.

18 Click the 🔍 ▾ **HTML Preview** button to see how your hyperlinks and anchors work when the page is published and viewed in a Web browser.

> 💡 The **Export as absolute URL** option lets your site visitors add your page as a bookmark. This is especially important if you use frames to display content within your site.

Notice that the titles you typed display when you hover the cursor over a hyperlink.

Close your browser when you have explored your new links.

For long Web pages with anchors towards the bottom of the page you may want to also offer a link back to the top of the page, often just called 'Top.' You don't need to use an anchor to do this. In the following steps we'll show you how.

19 Create a text object, type the word 'Top' and position it at the lower edge of the page. This will serve as our 'button.'

20 With the text object selected, click the 🐾 **Hyperlink** tool to add a hyperlink to the selected object.

In the **Hyperlinks** dialog, click the **Site Page** option. In the **Page name** drop-down list, choose your current page and click **OK**.

21 Preview your site to test this link.

We've just examined how to jump to specific points on a page, but hyperlinks can perform other tasks too...

22 Click the 🖼 **Import Picture** button. In the **Import Picture** dialog, browse to your **Workspace** folder. In a default installation, you'll find this in the following location:

C:\Program Files\Serif\WebPlus\X2\Tutorials\Workspace

- Select the **Ruin.png** image file.

- Select the **Link Picture** option.

- Click **Open**.

Back in the workspace, note that your cursor has changed to the ✛⬛ Picture Import cursor. You can single-click to import the picture at its original size, or click and drag to set the size of the picture.

Section 1

23 Click just under the **Section 1** heading at the left of the page and drag until the height of the picture spans half the distance between the **Section 1** and **Section 2** headings.

Release the mouse when you are happy with the image size.

24 With the image selected, press **Ctrl+K** to open the **Hyperlinks** dialog.

In the **Hyperlinks** dialog:

- Choose the **Picture** option.

- In the **Target Window or Frame** drop-down list, choose **New Window**.

- Click **OK**.

25 Preview your site to see this hyperlink option in action, clicking on the picture thumbnail to link to the full-size image.

> 💡 You can set image **Title** options—text that appears when you hover over the image—within the **Image Export Options** dialog. For more information, see the "Getting Started: Importing Images" tutorial.

You can use this 'self-linking picture' hyperlink method to build an online image gallery displaying thumbnails that viewers can click on to view the full size image.

When our site was published to a temporary folder for previewing purposes, WebPlus noticed that our resized 'thumbnail' was much smaller than the original image, so it created a much smaller version to make our page download more quickly.

26 Go back to your project, right-click the small image and choose **Properties.** You'll see that the thumbnail image is much smaller then the original image (in our case, 86 x 128 pixels).

This gives a file size difference of 27827 bytes compared to the original size of 301504 bytes of the original 570 x 852 pixel image. This is far more efficient and makes for a much faster download!

We'll leave you to explore the other hyperlink types—they are more self-explanatory in their nature, linking to other Web addresses, email addresses, other pages in your site, and so on.

Hyperlinks and anchors can be viewed and managed from the **Site Manager**, which you can access from the context toolbar.

For more information on using Site Manager, see online Help.

Importing Images

In the "Getting Started: Working With Text" tutorial, we discussed the various ways in which you can deliver text to viewers' screens quickly and efficiently. In this tutorial, we'll demonstrate that images too can appear quickly if optimized.

We'll introduce you to importing, placing, and managing images on your Web site. Along the way, we'll also highlight some useful dos and don'ts.

In this exercise, you will:

- Import and place images on the page.
- Learn about image resolution and resizing.
- Create self-linking picture hyperlinks.
- Apply a transparency effect to an image.
- Apply a monochrome effect to an image.
- Learn about file formats, site properties, and Web export options.

Importing Images

1   From the Startup Wizard, choose **Create > Start New Site**, or
    on the **File** menu, click **New**.

2   On the Tools toolbar, click 🖼 **Import Picture**.

    In the **Import Picture** dialog:

    • Browse to the **Workspace** folder. In a default installation, you'll
      find this in the following location:

      C:\Program Files\Serif\WebPlus\X2\Tutorials\Workspace

    • Select the **Lighthouse.jpg** file and then click **Open**.

Your cursor
changes to the
⊕🖼 Picture
Import cursor.

Single-click on
your page to
import the
image at its
native size.

3   Repeat step 2,
    this time
    clicking and
    dragging to add
    a smaller
    version of the
    image to the
    upper-right
    corner of your
    page.

💡 You can
also scale an
image at any
time by
selecting it
and dragging
its handles.

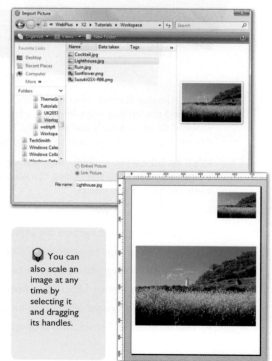

Upsampling and downsampling

The terms **downsampling** and **upsampling** are used to describe the rebuilding of images with either fewer or more pixels respectively.

An upsampled image has more pixels than the original, with the additional pixels added by clever mathematical guesswork. While it's impossible to make a low-quality image perfect, slight upsampling can smooth out some 'jagginess' in low-resolution images.

When an image has been reduced in size on the page, WebPlus generally downsamples automatically at publication time, outputting a reduced-resolution image that fits the space allocated to it on the page.

4   On the Standard toolbar, click to expand the ✎ ▾ **HTML Preview** drop-down list and click **Preview in Window**.

5   Right-click each image in turn and click **Image Properties**. Notice the difference in the reported file sizes of the two images. (Note also that the files are no longer called Lighthouse.jpg. This is because WebPlus has created new versions of the image.)

Both pictures use the same source image, but WebPlus has resampled the smaller version to recreate it using fewer pixels, so your page will download more quickly.

But suppose you want your site's visitors to be able to view high-resolution images while keeping the page size small. Here's an excellent approach:

6   Return to the WebPlus workspace. Delete the larger image then right-click over the small image and choose **Hyperlink**.

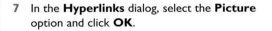

7   In the **Hyperlinks** dialog, select the **Picture** option and click **OK**.

8 In the  **HTML Preview** drop-down list, click **Preview in <your Web browser of choice>**.

Hover the mouse over the image—the cursor changes to a hand. Click to see a full-size version of the image.

9 Close the browser preview when you have finished experimenting.

This 'self-linking picture' hyperlink method is a favoured way of offering images to your site's visitors—the smaller image is quick to download for faster-loading pages, and only those viewers who want to see the full size image need click to download it. This eliminates unnecessary downloading for the rest of your visitors!

Now let's move on and discuss a few more hints and tips...

10 Select the image and then click the **Transform** tab (located in the lower right section of the workspace).

In both the 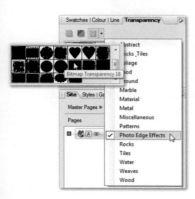 **Scale Width** and **Scale Height** text boxes, type '100' to reset the image to its native dimensions.

> **The Transform tab**
>
> The **Transform** tab provides controls for dynamically fine-tuning object placement and properties. The controls are context-sensitive and are displayed according to the type of object you've selected—shapes, images, and text can all be transformed. For details, see online Help.

In general, full-size images are published 'as is' in their original form (though with a different file name). But this is not always the case.

11 With the image selected, click the **Transparency** tab and expand the **Bitmap** drop-down list.

- Select the **Photo Edge Effects** category and then click **Bitmap Transparency 18**.

12 Click the  **HTML Preview** button to preview the site.

Let's now see how these changes have affected the way in which WebPlus publishes the image.

13 In your Web browser, right-click on the image and choose **Properties**.

Note the image size (189196 bytes in our case). This is different to the reported size of our original image, placed in step 2 (199277 bytes).

The use of transparency on our image means that WebPlus must achieve the effect by creating and publishing a modified image.

Other effects and operations that will cause recreation of an image include: cropping, rotation, most filter effects, recolouring, and significant overlaps of other objects.

Let's now take a look at the Picture context toolbar, which automatically displays at the top of the workspace whenever you have an image selected on your page.

Replace Picture ✍ Edit in PhotoPlus 🔍 ⤢ ⟳ ⟲ ⟳ ⟲ ⤢ ⤢ / Image Adjustments ▦ Frame Properties ⤢ Position Image ❶ Properties

You can use this toolbar's various command buttons to improve the appearance of an image by adjusting properties such as contrast, brightness, and colour. Let's try this now...

14 Click the 🖼 **Import Picture** button and add another copy of the **Lighthouse.jpg** image on to your page.

15 With the image selected click the 🖼 **Re-colour Picture** button on the Picture context toolbar.

16 In the **Fill** dialog, click a black colour swatch and then click **OK**.

Try experimenting with other colours, for example, create a sepia tone effect by applying a brown or dark orange fill colour.

Finally, we'll discuss another consideration when importing images and using drawn objects or 'fancy' text—**image formats**.

Imported images can have a variety of image formats (WebPlus supports the import of many different image formats), but most current Web browsers can only display **GIFs**, **JPGs**, and **PNGs**.

Images imported in one of these three Web-friendly formats may be published in their original format, untouched by WebPlus's intelligent image converter.

When necessary, WebPlus converts objects and images into a suitable format.

However, for drawn objects, modified artistic text, and imported images, you can set the individual or global image conversion options for your preferred published results.

Image compression formats

PNG is a 'lossless' format, which means that the quality does not suffer at the hands of built-in compression when the image is created.

JPEG/JPG files can be smaller than PNGs but JPEG compression can adversely affect quality.

GIF supports a single level of transparency (each pixel is either on or off) but the file format is restricted by only supporting 256 colours, which is fine for simple graphics but often unsuitable for photos.

For more information on the various file types, see online Help.

Let's see how you can modify both global and individual image export settings, starting with global settings.

17 On the **File** menu, click **Site Properties**.

In the **Site Properties** dialog, the **Graphics** tab offers global options for handling graphics when publishing your site.

In general:

- JPGs will be exported as JPGs.

- Generated graphics (drawn objects, text with non-solid fills, objects with transparency or filter effects, or cropped/rotated objects) will be exported as PNG for best quality.

- All other images will be 'recreated' as PNGs, unless WebPlus can reuse the original file.

18 Click **OK** to close the **Site Properties** dialog.

19 Right-click on your image and choose **Image Export Options**.

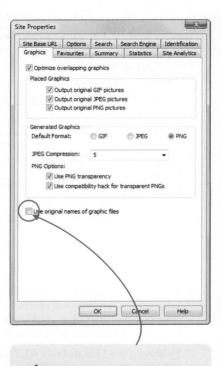

Note that when the original file is used, it will be renamed unless you select the **Use original names of graphic files** check box.

In the **Image Export Options** dialog, on the **Image Export Options** tab, you can override the global image publishing options by defining an image format for the selected object.

> For the ultimate in finding the right balance between file size and image quality for your site's images, consider exporting them from a program that offers a full **Export Optimizer** with export quality and file size preview, such as Serif PhotoPlus.

On the **Alt and Title** tab, you can enter pop-up TITLE and ALT text.

- TITLE text is the tooltip text that will appear when site visitors hover over the image in their Web browsers. This text is often used when clicking on a image has some function, for example, opening a larger version of the image in a new window.

- ALT text, used to describe the content and/or purpose of an image, is the text that will appear in the area of your page where the image will download. (Note that ALT text should *not* be used for images whose only purpose is decorative.)

  By default, the **Use default ALT text** option is selected. This tells WebPlus to use the TITLE text as the ALT description so that you only have to enter it once.

In order to accurately reproduce your design as a Web page, it is possible that items you create in WebPlus will be published as images. To allow for this, ALT & TITLE options are available for regular WebPlus objects as well as imported images.

For more information, see "Setting Picture Export Options" in online Help.

TITLE text can sometimes look a little messy on images and as such, should only be used when needed.

Enter the ALT text (shows while this picture is downloading and is used by screen readers and search engine robots):

☐ Use default ALT text

Ruin with Stormy Sky

You can create ALT text without adding TITLE text by clearing the **Use default ALT text** option.

We suggest that you experiment with TITLE and ALT text and preview your results. ALT text is an important consideration when making your site accessible to as many people as possible, and it may even help improve your site's rankings in search engine results.

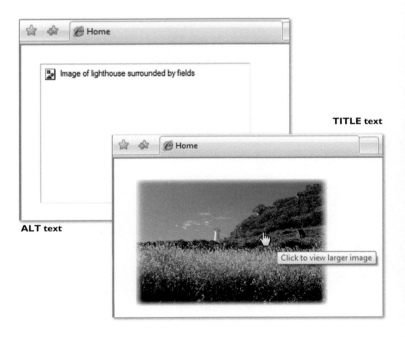

TITLE text

ALT text

In this tutorial, we've explored some image import options, some efficiency and quality issues, and some publishing considerations.

Related tutorials and projects include: "Getting Started: Creating Hyperlinks," "Getting Started: Building a Web Site," and "Getting Started: Creating Web-Friendly Sites."

Using Theme Graphics and the Gallery

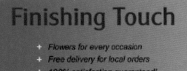

WebPlus X2 includes a wide range of theme graphics and gallery items—pre-designed objects that you can add to your site by simply clicking and dragging them from the Studio tabs.

If you're unfamiliar with Web site structure, we suggest you review the basic concepts before beginning this tutorial. See "Understanding site structure and navigation" in online Help or the "Getting Started: Introducing WebPlus X2" tutorial.

In this exercise, you'll learn how to:

- Add new pages to a site and rearrange site structure.
- Work with master page elements.
- Browse the Theme Graphics tab.
- Add and customize navigation and design elements.
- Add a Flash™ banner from the Gallery tab.
- Work with the User Details dialog.
- Switch theme graphic sets and update elements.
- Edit theme graphic settings.
- Work with WebPlus colour schemes.

Using Theme Graphics and the Gallery

In the first section of this tutorial, we'll create a new site, then we'll add some interactive **navigation elements** from the **Theme Graphics** tab. In the second section, we'll add some static **design elements** and show you how to customize them.

I: Adding navigation elements

1   Click **File**, then **New** (or from the Startup Wizard, select **Create > Start New Site** to create a new site with a single page.

First, we'll add some more pages to provide a basic structure for our viewers to navigate through.

2   Click the **Site** tab, select the **Home** page, and then click the ⊞ **Insert Page** button six times so you have seven pages in your site. (In the **Insert** dialog, accept the default page settings each time.)

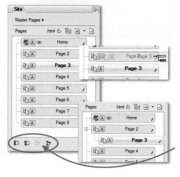

3   To make Page 3 a child of Page 2, click on Page 3 and then drag it up and slightly to the right of Page 2.

The cursor changes to indicate the new position of the page relative to the page onto which it is being dragged. Release the mouse button when the cursor changes to 🔲.

You can also move pages around using the buttons at the bottom of the tab (provided the upper **Master Pages** pane is collapsed.)

4   Click and drag the pages to make Pages 5 and 6 children of Page 4, and Page 7 a child of Page 6. Your finished site structure tree should look like ours.

> 💡 Arranging your content in a logical, structured way makes it easier for visitors to navigate. (If you need to review site structure, see the "Getting Started: Introducing WebPlus X2" tutorial.)

Although our site has no content, we'll assume our structure is in place and move on. Our first task is to set a colour scheme for our site.

5   On the context toolbar, click ◇ Colour Scheme . In the **Scheme Manager** dialog, on the **Schemes** tab, click the **Atlantis** scheme to apply it to your site.

    That's all we need to do for now; we'll return to colour schemes later.

6   At the top of the **Site** tab, click the **Master Pages** button to display the master pages used in this site—in this case there's just one master page shared by all the pages.

7   Double-click the **Master A** icon.

    Now we can edit the master page— the underlying background layer. Once we've added a navigation bar (navbar) to this master page you'll see how it all works.

8   At the top of the **Theme Graphics** tab, click the arrow to expand the drop-down category list.

You can use either the upper Categories tree or the lower Theme Graphics gallery to browse theme graphics. Having selected the top category, Theme Graphics, you now have three options available to you:

- **Current Site**—to view existing theme elements already in use.

- **Sets**—to view elements grouped into design collections.

- **Types**—to view elements by object function (for example, all buttons, all navigation bars, etc.).

9 In the upper Categories tree, click to expand the **Sets** category.

Here, theme graphics are grouped into sets with names such as 'Bright,' Dream,' 'Gel,' and so on.

Each set consists of various types of elements: static design elements like Bullets and Headings and interactive navigation elements like Buttons and Navigation Bars.

10 Using either the Categories tree or the lower Theme Graphics gallery, browse the list of sets and click the **Candy** set.

The gallery displays the **Candy** theme graphic set. Each thumbnail shows the element's type as a caption.

11 Click the **Horizontal Navbar** thumbnail and drag it on to the master page.

The navbar has three buttons—Home, Page 2, and Page 4. These top-level pages have been included in the navbar by default.

💡 You can also insert navbars and theme graphics using the ▤ **Insert Navigation Bar** and ▤ **Insert Theme Graphic** buttons from the Theme Graphics flyout, on the Web Objects toolbar.

12 Click to expand the 🌐 ▾ **HTML Preview** drop-down list and choose **Preview Site in <your Web browser of choice>**.

In your browser, hover your cursor over the navbar menu items.

Hover over the Page 2 button to pop up a menu that lets you access Page 3. Hover over Page 4 to access Pages 5 and 6. You can access Page 7 from a flyout from the Page 6 menu item.

These navigation options mirror the site structure we set up earlier.

13 Return to WebPlus when you have explored the navbar's behaviour.

14 On the **master p**age, right-click the navbar and click **Edit Navigation Bar**.

15 In the **Navigation Bar Settings** dialog, on the **Navigation Type** tab:

> By adding a single navbar element to the 'background' master page that's shared by all pages in the site, we save ourselves the trouble of placing a separate navbar on each page.
>
> You can place theme graphics on individual pages when appropriate, but remember that when any navigation element is on a master page, it behaves as if it's on the page itself!

- Select the **Same Level** navigation type.

- Select the **Include home page** and **Include parent page** check boxes.

- Click the **Popup Menu Properties** tab.

The **Popup Menu Properties** tab offers a host of visual formatting options.

For example, to prevent the navbar buttons from displaying popup menus for child pages, clear the **This navigation object has menus** option.

For now, leave the menus switched on and click **OK**.

Even though the navbar is still on the master page, its appearance will now vary depending on which page you're viewing. Let's take a look...

16 Double-click page entries on the **Site** tab (or single-click them in the Page Locator at the lower left of the workspace) to display each of the pages in turn.

As you move between pages, compare which buttons are present to the position of each page in the Site Structure tree. You'll see that in all cases, the button links are just as we specified; to 'sibling' pages on the same level, and to Home and Parent pages.

17 Click the arrow on the 🐾 ▾ **HTML Preview** button and this time select **Preview in Window** to display the site in an internal window.

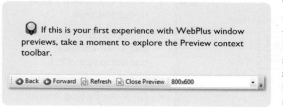

💡 If this is your first experience with WebPlus window previews, take a moment to explore the Preview context toolbar.

The navbars and menus enable you to get around the (mostly empty) site, but you can also use the Page Locator for navigation.

To return to the main window, click its tab (located at the top of the page, just below the toolbars) or close the preview window.

In designing an actual site, you might not set up a navbar with these particular links, but you've certainly had a glimpse of the possibilities. To close this tutorial, let's take a quick look at some other navigation element types. By now you'll have no trouble understanding how they work.

18 Return to the **Theme Graphics** tab to view the **Candy** theme set (as described in steps 8 to 10).

Make sure you are on the master page and then (one at a time) drag a **Previous Button** and **Next Button** on to your page, spacing them well apart.

Select both objects by dragging a selection bounding box around them with the ⬉ **Pointer** tool.

19 On the Arrange toolbar, click the ⊞ **Align Objects** button. In the **Align Objects** dialog, choose **Centre Vertically** and **Space evenly across**. Click **OK**.

Preview the site again to test the behaviour of these new elements.

20 If you haven't already done so, you should save your work before continuing.

The buttons we have added are each programmed to behave as their names imply: they link to adjacent 'sibling' pages on the same level. The navigational behaviour of these buttons isn't customizable, but their appearance—like that of all theme graphics—most certainly is.

So far, we've focused on **interactive navigation elements**, but you've also learned a lot that applies to theme graphics in general: about sets and types, how to select theme graphics and place them on a page or master page, and so on. If you explore the theme graphics sets further, you'll see that they also include **static design elements** like headings and bullets, which serve a decorative rather than functional role on the page.

In the following section, we'll continue building our site. We'll add a Flash™ banner from the **Gallery** tab and several design elements from the **Theme Graphics** tab. We'll also show you how to customize the appearance of these items once added to your site.

2: Adding and editing design elements

1 Open the master page of your site and click the **Gallery** tab.

2 At the top of the tab, expand the **WebPlus Gallery** folder, and then expand **Template Flash Banners**.

3 Expand the **1 Image** category and click on the **Slide in with Flicker** subcategory. The lower section of the tab now displays thumbnails of the various banner styles available.

4 Click and drag the **Flower Shop** thumbnail onto your master page.

5   Select the banner then
    on the **Align** tab, click
    🔲 **Centre
    Horizontally**.

Currently, the title of the
banner displays the company title that is set in the WebPlus **User
Details** dialog.

Unless you have already edited the user details, the title displayed by
default will be **Company Name**.

You can change this text by either updating the user details, or by
editing the Flash banner. We'll show both methods.

To update the banner title by setting user details

1   Click outside of the page area to deselect everything, then on the
    Page context toolbar, click 👓 Set User Details.

2   In the **User Details**
    dialog, change the
    company name to any
    name of your choice and
    then click **Update**.

    The banner updates with
    your new company name.

The **User Details** dialog is great for updating some text elements on
your banner, such as your company name, address, or telephone
number. But suppose you want to change the image—for example, to
display a new product—or edit the bullet points to reflect recent new
features or special offers. Let's do this now.

Take advantage of the **User Details** dialog to store frequently-used or frequently-updated information so you don't need to keep re-entering it—for example, think how often a mobile phone number or email address may change over time! The dialog lets you review all your details at a glance, and will update fields used in your site automatically.

To insert a user details field:

1 Create a text frame on your page.

2 On the **Insert** menu, choose **Information**, then click **User Details**.

3 In the **User Details** dialog, select the line of text you want to insert and then click **OK**.

To edit Flash banner elements

1 Double-click the banner, or right-click and select **Edit Flash**.

2 In the **Flash** dialog, in the **Parameters** pane, click to select the **CompanyName** element and then click the **Edit** button.

3 In the **Flash Parameters** dialog, in the **Value** box, delete the text (including the %) and type your company name. Click **OK**.

4 Repeat steps 2 and 3 to edit the bullet point text (line1, line2, and line3) as required.

5 When you've finished updating your text elements, click **OK** to cancel the **Flash** dialog and review your changes.

There may be times when you want to change other elements of your banner, such as the image, or even the colours.

You can use the same dialog to do this, as we'll now demonstrate.

6 Double-click the banner to open the **Flash** dialog.

7   In the right of the dialog, the
    Additional Files box lists the
    images used in the banner. (This
    particular banner only uses one
    image; others may use more.)

    Click the **Add** button and then
    browse to your
    Tutorials\Workspace folder. In a default installation, you'll find
    this folder in the following location:

    C:\Program Files\Serif\WebPlus\X2\Tutorials\Workspace

8   Select the
    Sunflower.png file
    and click **Open**.

    The new file is added
    to the **Additional
    Files** list.

> 💡 As this banner only uses one image, the image
> at the top of the list is the one that is displayed.
> You can, therefore, delete the other files listed in
> the **Additional Files** box if you wish.
>
> For banners using two or three images, the images
> are displayed in the order they are listed in the
> **Additional Files** box.
>
> To reorder the images, simply select a file in the
> list and then click **Up**. For more information, see
> the "Creating Personal Web Sites: Adding Flash
> Objects to your Site" tutorial.

9   Select the
    Sunflower.png file in
    the list and then click
    the **Up** button to
    move it to the top of
    the list.

10 Click **OK** to see your
    new image displayed in the banner.

11 Finally, drag your navbar below the
    angled dividing line on the banner.

Great, we're happy with
the way our banner
looks, so we'll now
switch back to the
Theme Graphics tab
and add some other
WebPlus design elements
to our master page.

> Because the navbar was created first,
> it will be behind the banner in the
> stacking order.
>
> To make it easier to work with, select
> the navbar and then on the Standard
> toolbar, click 🔲 **Bring to Front**.

To add Theme Graphic design elements

1   On the Theme Graphics tab, select the **Candy** set and drag a **Bullet
    I** element on to the left side of your page.

2   With the object selected,
    click **Edit**, then
    Replicate.

3   In the **Replicate** dialog:

    * In the **Replicate
      Method** section, select
      Create Line.

    * In the **Replicate
      Count** section, enter a
      Line Length of **4**.

    * In the **Spacing** section,
      select **Offset** spacing
      with **Horizontal** and **Vertical** settings of **0**
      and **100** pixels respectively.

    * Click **OK**.

    Back on your page, WebPlus creates a vertical
    'button bar' and selects all four bullet objects
    by default.

4   Drag your button bar into position on the left
    of your page.

5   Open **Page 2** in the workspace.

6 On the **Theme Graphics** tab, choose a theme set and drag a **Heading I** element on to the page.

HEADING TEXT

Theme Graphic Settings

Text | Font | Back Colour | Text Colour

☑ Specify text for this Theme Graphic

Our Products

7 Double-click the Heading element to open the **Theme Graphic Settings** dialog.

Our Products

8 On the **Text** tab, select the **Specify text for this Theme Graphic** check box, and type a new title for Page 2.

Click **OK** to accept the change.

We now have a basic layout with several navigation elements in place. The buttons on the bar can be made into hyperlinks to other pages in your site, other sites on the Internet, email addresses and more, but for now we'll leave them unlinked.

We'll now demonstrate switching themes sets, with and without altering the colour scheme.

First, let's return to the WebPlus colour schemes—a gallery of colour schemes that let you instantly revise the colours in your site.

9 On the Page context toolbar, click ◇ Colour Scheme .

In the **Scheme Manager** dialog, click the **Schemes** tab.

You'll see an assortment of named schemes. Our site uses the **Atlantis** theme (remember we set it previously), which is highlighted in the list.

10 Click a few different colour schemes.

As you select each new scheme, watch the **Preview** pane—you'll see various elements on the page (including theme graphics and the page background) change colour.

When you've finished experimenting with this 'paint-by-numbers' system, return to the **Atlantis** scheme.

> 🛈 It should be clear that the theme elements' coloration isn't fixed. It's variable because the objects have been marked to use particular numbered colours from whichever colour scheme is currently selected.
>
> You can read more about colour schemes in online Help.
>
> If you want to try creating your own colour scheme, perhaps from an image on your site, see the "Getting Started: Working with Colour Schemes" tutorial.

11 Click the **Theme Graphics** tab, and in the **Categories** tree click **Sets** to load the gallery with representative thumbnails showing each theme set.

In the gallery, locate the **Plastic** thumbnail and click on it.

You'll see the shape and design of the various theme graphics change. Elements of each set share a graphic theme, i.e., a similar 'look and feel.'

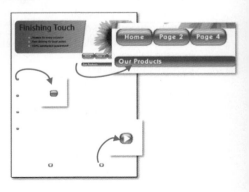

When you apply a different theme, you update all theme graphics to use the new theme's 'look.' As before, you can change the colour scheme of the objects by using the **Scheme Manager**.

12 Click **Edit**, then click **Undo Set Colour Scheme** to restore the original theme and scheme definitions. (Note that the Undo action also reverses the theme change.)

💡 If you find yourself too many 'Undos' away from where you started, a quick way to restore the site to its original state is to set the scheme back to **Atlantis** and then apply the **Candy** theme.

13 Switch to a different theme gallery and drag a new element onto the page. You'll see that the new element retains the appearance of its own theme, rather than adopting that of the elements already on the page. This allows you to mix and match navigation or design elements from different theme sets.

Note that the **Current Site** category of the **Object Themes** tab displays thumbnails for all the various theme graphics used in your site. These elements will each keep their 'theme of origin' characteristics unless you choose to change to another theme.

You can continue investigating other theme/scheme combinations if you wish. Notice that you can drill down one more level, into the gallery of elements for each set, and the first thumbnail there will let you apply the set as we've just been doing.

💡 You can right-click on a particular element's gallery thumbnail and choose to **Replace in Selection** or **Replace in Site**—options which give you both local and global control over elements of the identical type.

Let's now sum up what we have learned in this section of the tutorial...

- The Scheme Manager controls the colours used in all of your theme graphics.

- You can update all of your theme graphics in one step using the Theme Graphics sets.

- You can mix and match theme graphics from different sets.

- The Theme Graphics tab enables you to update individual or entire sets of elements in one go.

Well, that concludes this tutorial. We hope this exercise has convinced you of the versatility of theme graphics and gallery elements—especially navigation elements that not only adapt to your site structure but blend harmoniously with your site's visual design.

Equipped with a basic knowledge of these remarkable WebPlus features, you're ready to create your own Web site layouts. Now it's up to you and your imagination!

Theme graphic sets

As the word 'theme' implies, all the elements in a particular theme graphic set share similar design and colour attributes. By switching from one set to another, you can instantly update the appearance of any or all theme graphics in your site. Navigation elements are special because they 'understand' your site's page organization and structure.

Previewing and Publishing

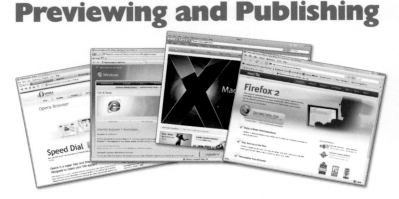

Having gone to some trouble to make a site—even simple sites take a certain amount of time and effort—you may want the world to see the fruits of your labour, which involves publishing your site on the Internet.

In this tutorial we will show you how to:

- Use the Preview toolbar to preview your site.

- Preview your site at different resolutions and in different Web browsers.

- Add new browsers to the WebPlus browser list.

- Publish and maintain your Web site.

> If you already have an Internet Service Provider (ISP), you will probably have space allocated for a personal Web site.
>
> For instructions on how to access this free Web space, see "Getting Started: Accessing Your Free Web Space."

Previewing and Publishing

1   From the WebPlus Startup Wizard, choose **Create > Start New Site**, and open the template of your choice.

2   Click the arrow to expand the 🔍 ▾ **HTML Preview** drop-down list. Click the first option, **Preview in Window**.

    You'll notice a delay while the page is exported from its WebPlus design origins to the language of the Web, HTML.

    Of course it's not only HTML language that describes the page that makes it look this way; WebPlus creates and organizes other files too, including images and special effects files such as animated marquees. Once exported, WebPlus displays the site preview in a built-in Microsoft Internet Explorer window.

3   To switch between your regular design view and the **Preview**, simply click on the tabs at the top of the workspace area.

    If you make any changes to your design, your site will be 'republished' when you next switch to the **Preview**. (You can also switch windows using the Window menu.)

    Note that the Preview context toolbar displays when you preview your site in WebPlus.

    From left to right, this toolbar offers:

*   **Back** and **Forward** buttons so you can undo and redo navigation commands that you carry out on your page using links and menus.

*   **Refresh** and **Close Preview** buttons.

*   **Preview size** drop-down list that allows you to see what your site will look like to visitors using different screen resolutions.

    This allows you to determine how much of your page width is visible at certain resolutions, and can help you to decide on page width and length, and position of navigation elements.

4   Click ☒ Close Preview .

5 Expand the **HTML Preview** drop-down list again and this time click the **Browser Preview List** option.

The **Browser Preview List** dialog opens, listing the browsers currently set up for previewing your WebPlus Web site.

It's up to you whether to download and install different browsers in order to preview your site through the eyes of other browser users.

The following steps are provided for illustrative purposes—but you're welcome to try them using any alternate browser of your choice.

Suppose you have downloaded and installed a version of Firefox and now wish to add it to WebPlus's browser list.

6 At the lower left of the **Browser Preview List** dialog, click **Auto Detect**.

A message box opens asking you if you are sure you want to proceed with Auto Detect as this operation will clear the current browser list.

Click **Yes** to proceed.

Firefox is automatically detected and added to the list.

7 Return to WebPlus and expand the **HTML Preview** drop-down list. WebPlus has detected Firefox and added it to the browser list. Click to preview your page in this browser.

There may be times when you want to manually add a browser to this list, for instance if the browser has not been automatically detected by WebPlus X2. Now let's suppose you have downloaded and installed the Safari Browser for previewing purposes... here's how you'd proceed:

8   Expand the **HTML Preview** drop-down list again and click the **Browser Preview List** option.

9   In the **Browser Preview List** dialog, click **Add**.

Add Browser	
Description:	Safari
File name:	Browse...
	OK Cancel

In the **Add Browser** dialog:

- In the **Description** box, type 'Safari.'

- Click **Browse**, browse to the folder where Safari is installed and select its executable file name (safari.exe).

- Click **Open**, then click **OK** twice to return to WebPlus.

10 Expand the **HTML Preview** drop-down list and click the **Browser Preview List** option. You'll now be able to preview your Web site in the Safari browser.

Previewing either the current page, or the whole site, in a range of browsers helps you to ensure that a larger number of Internet surfers can see the site as intended.

At the time of writing this tutorial, Internet Explorer (6 and 7 combined) is still the most popular Web browser, however, Mozilla Firefox now accounts for over a third share of the market. Other browsers such as Opera (especially for mobile devices) and Safari are also supported by WebPlus and should be taken into consideration. Such browsers may offer Web surfers speedier page loading or other functionality such as mouse gesture controls.

Mozilla   Internet   Safari   Opera
Firefox   Explorer

We'll assume that our design looks
great in a range of Internet browsers.
Now it's time to publish our site and
make our presence known on the
Internet. Even though you may have
saved your Web site as a WebPlus
project, it's not truly a 'Web site' until
you've converted it to HTML files and
graphics files in a form that can be
viewed in a Web browser. In WebPlus,
this conversion process is called
publishing.

> 🔵 Note that regardless of
> your browser, you won't be
> able to fully test navbar and
> other hyperlink
> functionality if you preview
> the current page, rather
> than the whole site.

WebPlus can publish your site in two ways:

- **To a disk folder** so you can use your site as a network-based
  Intranet; write it to CD-ROM for distribution; or upload it manually
  to an Internet server using file transfer protocol (FTP) software.

- **To the Web**, that is, directly to a Web server from WebPlus. To
  do this, you'll need a **host** for your Web site—disk space on a
  server connected to the Internet—so that others can access your
  site. This usually means opening an account with an Internet service
  provider (ISP).

  Typically, the big subscription networks allocate to each user several
  megabytes of server space for a 'personal Web site,' and many plans
  are available from smaller ISPs. Once you've set up your account and
  can connect your computer to the host, publishing to the Web is
  simply a matter of transferring files.

To publish to disk folder

1   Check your page names, file names, and picture export settings in
    the **File/Site Properties** and **Format/Web Export Options**
    dialogs.

    (For details, see "Setting page and file names" and "Setting picture
    export options" in online Help.)

2   On the Standard toolbar, click 🖾 **Publish to Disk Folder** (or
    click **File**, then **Publish Site**, then **Publish to Disk Folder**).

3 In the **Publish to Disk Folder** dialog:

- Click **Choose Folder** and browse to the folder where you wish to store the output files, or create a new folder. Click **OK**.

- In the **Page Range** tree, select which page(s) to publish (or select the **Publish All Pages** check box to publish all pages).

- Click **OK**.

WebPlus exports the selected pages and opens the **Web Site Publishing** dialog.

4 In the **Web Site Publishing** dialog, you can choose to:

- **View site in Web browser:** Opens a new instance of your designated Web browser on the first exported page of your site.

- **View this URL:** Avoid opening a new instance of your browser by selecting the URL for your site in the drop-down list.

- **View files in Windows Explorer**.

To publish to the Web

1 Check your page names, file names, and picture export settings in the **File/Site Properties** and **Format/Web Export Options** dialogs.

(For details, see "Setting page and file names" and "Setting picture export options" in online Help.)

2 On the Standard toolbar, click ▣ **Publish to Web** (or click **File**, then **Publish Site**, then **Publish to Web**).

3 In the **Publish to Web** dialog, click **Accounts**, then click **Add,** to open the **Account Details** dialog.

When publishing to the Web (or uploading it manually using FTP software) you'll need to provide the following information, most of which you can obtain from your Internet Service Provider (ISP) or Web host:

- **Account name:** A descriptive name for this connection. This can be any name of your choice. You'll use it to identify this account in WebPlus (you may have more than one).

- **FTP address:** The URL (path), similar to a Web address, that locates the Internet-based server that will store your files.

    This will start with 'ftp://' and is supplied by your service provider.

- **Port number:** Unless directed by your provider, leave the **Port number** set at 21. This is the default port used by most FTP servers for file transfer.

- **Folder:** Allows you to upload sites to sub-folders of your main Web site's address.

    You can leave this blank unless you are directed otherwise by your provider, or you want to publish to a specific subfolder of your root directory. (This may also be needed to correctly route your upload specifically to your own Web space,)

- **Username:** Pre-assigned by your provider, this is typically the same as your email login or the information used to identify your 'dial-up' or 'always-on' account.

You'll need this to log on to the FTP server to gain permission to upload files. It may also help to automatically route your upload to the correct location on the server. Usernames are often **case-sensitive** and if so must be entered exactly as specified by your ISP or Web host.

- **Password:** As for Username, this is normally the same information required for ISP or Web host account log-on, and is often case-sensitive.

- **Passive Mode:** When this option is **cleared**, WebPlus makes a single connection to the FTP provider or Web host and uses this connection to upload your Web pages and pass information back and forth.

  When this option is **selected**, WebPlus uses one connection to connect to the host and uses this to pass information about what is about to be uploaded. Subsequently, multiple additional connections are used to upload the content. This is generally the preferred (most efficient) method, and is selected by default.

- **Web site URL:** The URL of your Web site—this is the 'address' where your site resides on the Web.

4   When you've entered all your information, click **OK**.

In the **Manage FTP Accounts** dialog, your new FTP account and settings are displayed.

5   Click **Upload**, to return to the **Publish to Web** dialog.

6   In the **Page Range** tree, select which page(s) to publish and then click **OK**.

WebPlus will convert your design into HTML pages with associated graphics and other files, then begin to upload your site to the Internet, showing individual file progress and overall progress.

Note: Subsequent uploads of your site to that account will allow you to perform either an **Incremental Update** or a **Full Upload**.

The basic process of uploading files to a server is quite simple, as outlined above. However, some ISPs and Web hosts are better than others at providing the basic information you'll need the first time you publish to their server (ftp address, steps needed to connect to the server, any special requirements, and so on).

If you're having problems we suggest you check your provider's Web site to find the information you need, or contact their customer support team.

Note: Serif is not your service provider and cannot supply this information.

- **Incremental Update:** If you choose to perform an incremental upload, WebPlus will export your site and compare the exported files to those already on the server. It will only upload files that are new or have changed since the last upload. It can also be told to check for missing files.

- This makes it quick and easy to replace minor elements of your site!

- **Full Upload:** If you choose to perform a full upload, WebPlus will upload all the files, regardless of whether they have changed since the last upload.

In both cases you can instruct WebPlus to delete uploaded files that are no longer required by selecting this option in the dialog.

Having discussed preview and publish options, there's one more function you may wish to know about—Web site maintenance.

Once you've uploaded your Web site, WebPlus offers a way for you to rename, move, and delete files on your space of your Internet server (although doing so may 'break' navigation links or picture display in your site).

Let's see how it works...

• Click **File**, choose **Publish Site**, then click **Maintain Web Site**.

  The same account logon information is required in order to connect, but once connected you will be offered an Explorer-like interface with familiar controls and behaviour for file management.

  Although you may need to verify your upload details with your Internet Service Provider, the actual publishing process couldn't be much easier.

With multi-sized and multi-browser previews, incremental uploads, and site maintenance, WebPlus provides all the tools and features you need to get your Web site 'online.'

If your Web server cannot accommodate spaces in file names, complete the following steps to have WebPlus remove the spaces and symbols from file names when they are published:

1 On the **File** menu, click **Site Properties**.

2 Click the **Options** tab and then select the **Remove spaces** and **Remove symbol character** options.

Web pages are normally published with lower case file names. From the same dialog check **Make lower case** to get WebPlus to do this for you.

If you've already published your site, you'll need to republish to fix the problem. This also improves site reliability.

Accessing Your Free Web Space

If you already have an Internet Service Provider (ISP), you will probably have space allocated for a personal Web site. In our experience, however, the way to access this Web space is not always evident.

The following guide aims to provide you with the information you need to access free Web space provided by some of the most popular ISPs.

Note that while the following information was correct at time of publishing, some of it is subject to change. If you have questions, you should contact your provider.

> For general information on publishing your site (to disk or to the Web) and uploading Web pages to your ISP, see the "Getting Started: Previewing and Publishing" tutorial and online Help.

Accessing Your Free Web Space

This tutorial is divided into two sections:

- The first section assumes that your Internet Service Provider is Virgin Media and provides step-by-step instructions to show you how to upload your Web site to this particular ISP.

- The second section lists the information you will need to publish your site to some of the other popular ISPs: Virgin Media (blueyonder, ntl:), BT Yahoo!, Yahoo! Geocities, TalkTalk AOL, Orange, PIPEX (Pipex Communications), PlusNet, and Tiscali UK.

Uploading your site to Virgin Media

1 In the WebPlus workspace, on the Standard toolbar, click 🔲 **Publish to Web** (or click **File**, then **Publish Site**, then **Publish to Web**).

2 In the **Publish to Web** dialog, click **Accounts**, then click **Add,** to open the **Account Details** dialog.

3 In the **Account Details** dialog, enter the following information.

- **Account name:** A descriptive name for this particular connection in WebPlus. This name is chosen by you. We used 'Virgin Media.'

- **FTP address:** upload.ntlworld.com

- **Port number:** 21—port 21 is used by default by most FTP servers for file transfer.

- **Folder:** Leave this blank unless you want to publish to a specific subfolder of your root directory

- **Username:** Your virgin media internet user name *e.g. user.name*

- **Password:** Your virgin media internet password *e.g. s123456789*

- **Web site URL:** http://homepage.ntlworld.com/*user.name*

4 When you've completed your details, click **OK**.

Passive Mode

When this option is cleared, WebPlus makes a single connection to the FTP provider and uses this connection to upload your Web pages and pass information back and forth.

When this option is selected, WebPlus makes one connection to connect to the host and uses this to pass information about what is about to be uploaded. Subsequently, multiple additional connections are used to upload the content.

Passive mode is generally the most efficient method, and is therefore selected by default.

Account Details

Please enter your account details to access your FTP Web space.
Make sure your Username and Password are correct with exact and lowercase spelling.

Details

Account name:	Virgin Media
FTP address:	upload.ntlworld.com
Port number:	21 (Default FTP Port 21)
Folder:	(May be ca...
Username:	user.name
Password:	••••••••• ☑ Save pa...
Passive mode:	☑ (Uncheck this if you have problems c...
Web site URL:	.ntlworld.com/user.name (optional)

[OK] [Cancel]

In the **Manage FTP Accounts** dialog, your new FTP account and settings are displayed.

5 Click **Upload** to return to the **Publish to Web** dialog.

Manage FTP Accounts

FTP Account

Virgin Media

[Add...] [Copy...] [Edit] [Delete]

Settings

ftp://upload.ntlworld.com/

Username: user.name
Password: ••••••••••   [Test]

[Upload] [Close] [Help]

Publish To Web

FTP Account

Virgin Media   ▾ [Accounts...]

Server: upload.ntlworld.com
User name: user.name
Password: ••••••••••

Page Range

☐ Publish All Pages

☑ 🏠 Home   [Toggle Select]
  ▢ Page 2
    ▢ Page 3   [Toggle Branch]
  ▢ Page 4
    ▢ Page 5   [Select All]
  ▢ Page 6
    ▢ Page 7

☐ Back-up the document to the remote se...

Site Checker

[OK]

Uploading files

Server: www.serifwebresources.com
Remote directory: /tutorials/

File 1 of 29
Image swap with folder_image.swf
                              286.0 of 367.6 Kb

Overall progress:
33 Kb/Sec   Time remaining: 14 Sec

[Cancel]

6 In the **Publish to Web** dialog, in the **Page Range** tree, select the page(s) you want to publish (or select the **Publish All Pages** option) and then click **OK**.

WebPlus converts your design into HTML pages with associated graphics and other files, then connects to the server and uploads your files.

A dialog indicates the progress of the connection and upload process.

 Subsequent uploads of your site to that account will allow you to perform either an **Incremental Update** or a **Full Upload**.

- **Incremental Update:** If you choose to perform an incremental upload, WebPlus will export your site and compare the exported files to those already on the server. It will only upload files that are new or have changed since the last upload. This makes it quick and easy to replace minor elements of your site!

- **Full Upload:** If you choose to perform a full upload, WebPlus will upload all the files, regardless of whether they have changed since the last upload.

In both cases you can instruct WebPlus to delete uploaded files that are no longer required by selecting the **Delete unused remote files** option in the dialog.

Using other Internet Service Providers

If you're publishing your WebPlus site to an ISP Web server other than Virgin Media:

- Follow the steps outlined in the previous section, referring to the following list for special requirements, and when completing the **Account Details** dialog in step 3.

   In most cases, the information you enter is the same for all ISPs—for example, in the **Password** box you will type the password you use to log on to your ISP account.

   However, the **FTP address**, **Web site URL**, and in some cases **Folder** options, are specific to each provider.

   You may need to verify these details with your provider as they are subject to change. (It's also a good idea to record this information for future reference.)

blueyonder (Virgin Media)

WebPlus **Account Details** dialog options:

- **Account name:** Your choice, for example, 'blueyonder'

- **FTP address:** ftp://ftp.pwp.blueyonder.co.uk/

- **Port number:** 21

- **Folder:** Leave blank unless you want to publish to a specific subfolder of your root directory.

- **Username:** Your blueyonder username

- **Password:** Your blueyonder password

- **Web site URL:** http://www.*your username*.pwp.blueyonder.co.uk

  (Where '*your username*' is the username you use to log on to your blueyonder account.)

ntl: (Virgin Media)

WebPlus **Account Details** dialog options:

- **Account name:** For example, 'NTL'

- **FTP address:** ftp://upload.ntlworld.com

- **Port number:** 21

- **Folder:** Leave blank unless you want to publish to a specific subfolder of your root directory.

- **Username:** Your primary email account name

- **Password:** Your primary email account password

- **Web site URL:**
  http://homepage.ntlworld.com/*your primary username*

  (Where '*your primary username*' is the primary username you use to log on to your ntl: account. This is normally the first part of your email address (e.g. if your email address is joe.smith@ntlwordl.com, your username would be joe.smith.)

Yahoo! Geocities

WebPlus **Account Details** dialog options:

- **Account name:** For example, 'Yahoo! Geocities'
- **FTP address:** ftp.geocities.com
- **Port number:** 21
- **Folder:** Leave blank unless you want to publish to a specific subfolder of your root directory.
- **Username:** Your Yahoo! ID
- **Password:** Your Yahoo! ID password
- Web site URL: http://geocities.com/*your Yahoo! ID*

(Where '*your Yahoo! ID*' is the primary username you use to log on to your Yahoo! account.)

BT Yahoo!

You must connect to the Internet via your BT Yahoo! connection before beginning the upload process.

WebPlus **Account Details** dialog options:

- **Account name:** For example, 'BT Yahoo'
- **FTP address:** ftp.uk.geocities.com or ftp.btinternet.com
- **Port number:** 21
- **Folder:** Leave blank unless you want to publish to a specific subfolder of your root directory.
- **Username:** Your primary BT Yahoo! Username
- **Password:** Your primary BT Yahoo! Password
- Web site URL: http://geocities.com/*your primary username*

(Where '*your primary username*' is the primary username you use to log on to your BT Yahoo! account.)

PIPEX

You must activate your PIPEX Web space before you can upload to it. To do this, log on at www.pipex.com and then choose **Control Panel**.

WebPlus **Account Details** dialog options:

- **Account name:** For example, 'PIPEX'
- **FTP address:** ftp://dslftp.dsl.pipex.com
- **Port number:** 21
- **Folder:** Leave blank unless you want to publish to a specific subfolder of your root directory.
- **Username:** Your PIPEX username
- **Password:** Your PIPEX password
- **Web site URL:** http://www.*your username*.dsl.pipex.com/

(Where '*your username*' is the username you use to log on to your PIPEX account.)

Orange

You must set up and activate your Orange Web space prior to use. To do this, follow the instructions found at http://www.orange.co.uk/sitebuilder/ftp.htm. WebPlus acts as an FTP transfer package, so this is the router that needs to be assumed.

WebPlus **Account Details** dialog options:

- **Account name:** For example, 'Orange'
- **FTP address:** sitebuilder.wanadoo.co.uk
- **Port number:** 21
- **Folder:** Leave blank unless you want to publish to a specific subfolder of your root directory.
- **Username:** Your Orange username followed by the sitename created in FTP My Site e.g. william@shakespeare.orange.co.uk/sitename
- **Password:** Your Orange login password
- **Web site URL:** http://mysite.orange-members.co.uk/sitename

PlusNet

WebPlus **Account Details** dialog options:

- **Account name:** For example, 'PlusNet'
- **FTP address:** ftp://ftp.plus.net
- **Port number:** 21
- **Folder:** htdocs
- **Username:** Your PlusNET username
- **Password:** Your PlusNET password
- **Web site URL:** http://www.*your username*.plus.com

  (Where '*your username*' is the username you use to log on to your PlusNet account.)

Tiscali UK

1   You must connect to the Internet via your Tiscali connection before beginning the upload process.

2   You must activate your Web space before you can upload to it. To do this, click the **My account** link on the Tiscali Home page. For details, go to www.tiscali.co.uk.

WebPlus **Account Details** dialog options:

`tiscali.`

- **Account name:** For example, 'Tiscali'
- **FTP address:** ftp://ftp.myweb.tiscali.co.uk
- **Port number:** 21
- **Folder:** Leave blank unless you want to publish to a specific subfolder of your root directory.
- **Username:** Your Tiscali login name or email address, in lower case. Note that this must include '@tiscali.co.uk'
- **Password:** Your Tiscali login password—this is case-sensitive
- **Web site URL:** http://myweb.tiscali.co.uk/*name*

  (Where '*name*' corresponds to the name you gave to your Web space during the activation stage.)

TalkTalk

You need to set up your WebSpace account to be able to upload WebPlus pages. To do this visit http://supportcentre.talktalk.net/ and login. From here you may use the WebSpace tab to create a new account and give your Web site an individual name.

WebPlus **Account Details** dialog options:

- **Account name:** For example, 'TalkTalk'

- **FTP address:** www.yourwebsite.talktalk.net - Where *yourwebsite* is the name created on the support centre page

- **Port number:** 21

- **Folder:** Leave this blank unless you want to publish to a specific subfolder of your root directory.

- **Username:** *yourwebsite*

- **Password:** the password as set up on the webspace account creation

- **Web site URL:** http://www.yourwebsite.talktalk.net

AOL (TalkTalk)

WebPlus **Account Details** dialog options:

- **Account name:** For example, 'AOL.'

- **FTP address:** members.aol.com

- **Port number:** 21

- **Folder:** Leave this blank unless you want to publish to a specific subfolder of your root directory.

- **Username:** anonymous

- **Password:** Your full AOL email address

- **Web site URL:** http://members.aol.com/*your AOLscreenname*

(Where '*your AOLscreenname*' is the screenname you use to log on to AOL.)

💡 We've tried to cover the most popular Internet Service Providers available today, but you may be using a provider that is not listed.

Some service providers are better than others at providing the basic information you'll need the first time you publish to their server (ftp address, steps needed to connect to the server, any special requirements, and so on).

If you're having problems accessing the Web space provided by your ISP or Web host, you should check their Web site or contact their customer support team.

Once you have the information you need, you should record it for future reference.

Note: Serif is not your service provider and cannot supply this information.

We hope you've found this information useful and are now able to access your Web space and upload your WebPlus files! If your ISP does not give you free Web space, don't worry, there are many alternative sources out there.

One of the best ways to find these is by navigating to your favourite search engine using your Web browser and searching for "free Web space."

As a quick reference, however, some of the more popular free Web hosts include the following:

* http://geocities.yahoo.com/
* http://www.fortunecity.com/
* http://www.tripod.lycos.com/

These hosts provide at least 20 MB of storage, which should be more than adequate for your WebPlus sites.

Introducing HTML

```
<head>
<meta http-equiv="Content-Type" content="text
<meta name="Generator" content="Serif WebPlus
<title>Home</title>
<style type="text/css">
<!--
body {margin: 0px; padding: 0px;}
-->
</style>
```

While WebPlus is an extremely versatile and feature-rich publishing tool, there are features and functions, that may require you to add some HTML code of your own.

For example, you can add HTML code to achieve functionality that WebPlus does not natively support, or elements—like the sample hit counter we'll demonstrate here—that involve some personalization for your site or your needs.

In this tutorial we'll show you how you can use HTML code fragments to enhance and customize your Web site. You'll learn how to:

- Insert HTML code fragments.
- Add a simple hit counter script to your Web site.

The WebPlus **Smart Objects** include hit counters, active viewers, blogs, shout boxes, polls, and more, which you can quickly and easily insert on your site. Just sign up with Serif Web Resources and you're on your way—no code necessary!

For more information, see the online Help.

For step-by-step instructions, see the "Adding Dynamic Content to Your Site" tutorial, in the Creating Personal Web Sites section.

Introducing HTML

1 From the WebPlus Startup Wizard, select **Create > Use Design Template**.

2 Select any Web site template and click **Open**.

3 Use My Computer/Windows Explorer to browse to your **Workspace** folder. In a default installation, you'll find this in the following location:

   C:\Program Files\Serif\WebPlus\X2\Tutorials\Workspace

4 Double-click on the **Sample counter code.txt** file to open it. It may open in Notepad or another text editor.

   Select all of the text (try pressing **Ctrl+A** on your keyboard) and copy it to your Clipboard by pressing **Ctrl+C**. Close the text editor program and return to WebPlus.

5 On the Web Objects toolbar, click ⊕ **Insert HTML Code**, then click on the page or pasteboard area to create a new HTML Code Fragment window at default size (or drag to adjust the dimensions of the window).

   > 🛈 When the **Ignore page position (raw HTML)** check box is cleared, WebPlus tries to incorporate your HTML code fragment in the correct location (where you place it on your page) when your site is published.

6 In the **Attach HTML Code** dialog, click the **Paste to Body** button.

   WebPlus inserts the Clipboard text into the body of the file.

7 Click **OK** to close the dialog.

8 On the page, the code fragment is displayed in the HTML Code Fragment window.

HTML Code Fragment
```
<!-- Gostats.com web hit code. Please do not change th
<script type="text/javascript">var go_mem="dcookserif
<script type="text/javascript" src="http://c3.gostats.co
<noscript>
<a href="http://c3.gostats.com/gogi/viewstats.pl?mn=
<img src="http://c3.gostats.com/gogi/count.pl?mn=dc
</noscript><br>
<a href="http://gostats.com">free hit counter</a>
<!-- End of Gostats.com web hit code -->
```

9 To see your new hit counter as it will be displayed to your site visitors, click the 🔍 ▾ **HTML Preview** button and choose to **Preview Site in <your browser of choice>**.

252745

free hit counter

If you are connected to the Internet while you are previewing this sample site, the counter code will connect to a server and update the hit count, then feed this number back to your site as a small image.

ℹ️ We had to sign up for an account, which was free in this case, so that the Web Counter service provider could uniquely identify hits to our site. Each time the code is viewed in a browser, the Web Counter service provider's HTML and JavaScript code increments the count—so by completing this tutorial you will raise our sample site's count (if you are online)!

In our example, the HTML code is pasted in the HTML Body section. Depending on the type of HTML object you're planning to include, you may need to paste code into the Head, Body, or both sections. It's usually not difficult to figure out what to put where.

The HTML code itself will include <HEAD></HEAD> and/or <BODY></BODY> tag pairs that demarcate these blocks.

If some of the code is required to be pasted into the HTML Head section, it will often be noted as a 'comment' in the code.

In HTML, comments are enclosed inside <!-- --> characters. Comments are essentially ignored by the Web browser and are there to provide memory aids, information or instructions to the person viewing or writing the code. Comments are often great ways of including things like the Web designers name and copyright information.

To view the source code on any Web page, right-click the page and choose view source from the menu.

We've just shown you how to add a hit counter as an object, but to get one that actually registers hits on a real Web page, you'll need to sign up with a service.

> The text file we opened contains HTML and JavaScript (another flavour of Web-language) code obtained from a Web Counter service.

More information

A hit counter is just one example of HTML or JavaScript code that can enhance your Web site. However, there is a lot more that you can do. Take a look at sites like

- HTML Goodies (www.htmlgoodies.com)
- JavaScript City (www.javascriptcity.com)
- HotScripts.com (www.hotscripts.com)

for code-oriented tutorials, script ideas, and sample code that you can consider for your sites! (Please note that Serif is not responsible for content found on external sites.)

Building a Web Site Using WebPlus X2

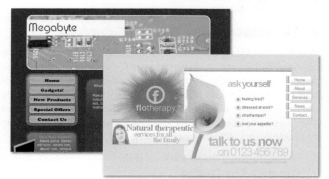

WebPlus X2 provides you with a wide range of powerful tools and building blocks that you can use to create your own Web site.

In this tutorial, we'll highlight the various ways you can build a site using predesigned WebPlus elements—which we'll show you how to customize to suit your needs.

We'll work with the following:

- Web Site templates
- Theme graphics
- The WebPlus gallery
- Colour schemes
- Sample Web sites

Building a Web Site

This tutorial is divided into three sections to make it easier for us to explain, and for you to follow. However, while each section focuses on a different WebPlus design 'tool,' it's important to note that you can combine these tools when working on your own Web site designs.

> If theme graphics are new to you, we suggest you take a look at the "Getting Started: Using Theme Graphics and the WebPlus Gallery" tutorial before working through this project.

1: Templates and Theme Graphics

WebPlus includes a selection of predesigned templates, which are intended to be used as starting points for your own sites. These templates were designed using a range of WebPlus tools—colour schemes, theme graphics and other gallery elements—providing you with countless possibilities for customization. In this section, we'll take a Web site template and show you just a few of the ways you can adapt it to produce very different end results.

1 In the Startup Wizard, click **Create > Use Design Template**.

2 In the **Create New Site From Template** dialog, browse to select the **Megabyte** thumbnail and click **Open**. (Remember that your can zoom into any template by clicking 🔍.)

This is a simple site containing four main pages, accessed via the vertical navbar running down the left of the page.

On the **Site** tab, these four top-level pages are listed, along with two pages that are not included in the navigation: **Privacy Policy** and **Terms of Use**.

This template provides the basic structure and layout we want to use in our own site. However, there are certain elements we'd like to change and pages that we would like to add. Fortunately, due to the wide range of customizable WebPlus elements, many of our changes can be achieved really easily!

Adding a search field

A really useful feature on any site is a search field that allow your visitors to quickly find something on your site. In WebPlus the search tool has two separate elements, the search text box and the results field. Let's add one to our site.

1   The search text box will be most useful if it can be accessed from any page. This means that we need to put it on the site's master page. View the master page by choosing it from the **Page Locator**.

2   From the **Web Objects** toolbar choose the **Site Search** tool .

3   You will get a warning dialog to say that this will not work without the results box. Click **OK** as we will add this in a moment.

4   The cursor will change to ⁺▓. Click once on the page to add the Search box. Drag the object so that it is positioned just underneath the Megabyte header image.

5   The next step is to add the results box. We will give this its own page. In the **Site** tab click the down arrow on the ⊞ ▾ **Insert page** flyout. Choose **New Template Page** from the menu.

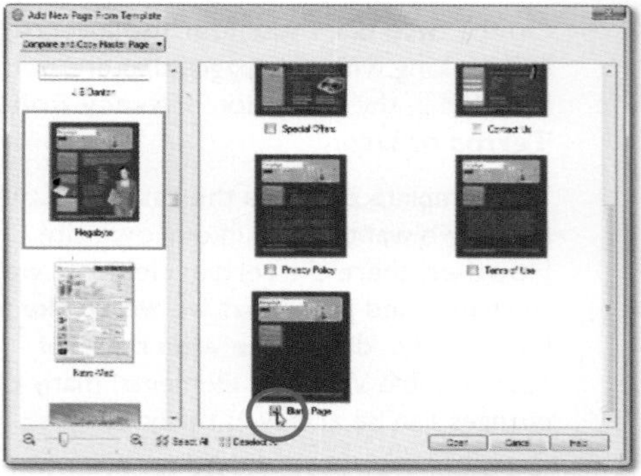

6   A dialog opens displaying
    the current template set
    with the Blank Page
    already selected. Click
    OK to add it to your site.

7   In the **Site** tab, click on
    the **Blank Page** and use
    the navigation buttons to
    move the page to the
    bottom of the list.

    If the buttons are not
    showing, make sure that
    you don't have your master
    pages open at the top of the tab.

8   Right-click the new page and click **Page Properties**.

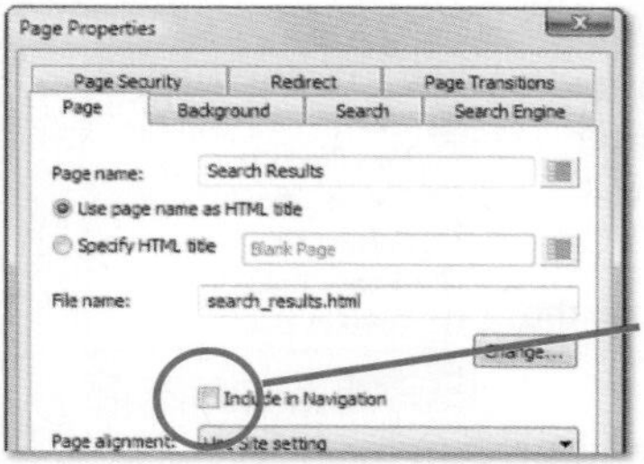

9   In the **Page Properties** dialog:

    •   Change the **Page name** to
        Search Results.

    •   Change the **File name** to
        search_results.html

    •   Uncheck the **Include in
        Navigation** option.

    •   Click **OK**.

10 In the **Site** tab, double click the Search Results
    page to open it.

11 From the ✎ ▾ **Site Search** flyout on the
    Web Objects toolbar, click ▦ .

12 Drag on the page to insert the object at the
    required size. We made it large enough to fill
    the blank space.

Notice that the placeholder text is very dark. This is because the results text uses the colour set for Scheme Colour 1 which in this scheme is very similar to that used for the background.

13 Right click on the Search Results object and choose **Edit Site Search Results object...** from the menu.

14 In the dialog, uncheck the **Use Scheme Colour** option and click the down arrow.

We chose a light grey but you can always click **More Colours...** for a larger selection.

Click **OK**.

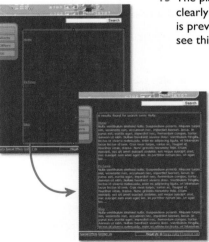

15 The placeholder text should now be clearly visible. All you have to do now is preview your site in a browser to see this new object in action!

Let's now add an offsite link to our site.

Adding an offsite link

We want to add a link to a related company that sells gadgets and other items. Instead of doing this with a hyperlink, we are going add an offsite link. Why? It means that the page will appear in our navbar as if it's a page on our site.

1   Right click on the **Home** page in the **Site** tab and choose **Insert Offsite Link...**.

2   In the dialog:

*   Choose **Internet Page**.

*   Enter the URL as

    http://www.gizoo.com

*   In the **Menu name** type **Gadgets!**

*   Change the **Type** to **New Window**.

*   Ensure that **Include in Navigation** is checked.

*   Click **OK**.

3   Your link should now appear in the **Site** tab below the Home page.

    If you preview the site and click on the Gadgets! item on the navbar, a new window should open displaying the Gizoo home page.

    Close the window when you have finished.

💡 **Offsite links**

Typically, offsite links are separate from your site—for example, linking to another Web site address that you want to include in your navigation structure (often in a popup menu). The offsite link appears in the Site Structure tree so you can manipulate it just as if it were a page in your site.

For information on creating offsite links, see "Adding, removing, and rearranging pages in online Help."

You may have noticed that the navbar has resized to contain all of the site pages but it no longer fits neatly inside the surrounding box. This is because it is a Theme Graphic element that is placed on top of some Quickshapes.

Let's resize the Quickshapes to fit and whilst we're there, we'll see if there is another navbar style that works better for our Web site.

Changing the style of the navbar

1   On the **Site** tab expand the **Master Pages** and double click **Master A** to view it.

2   Select the navbar object. When selected, it will be surrounded by a grey bounding box with a ⎍ T ⎍ button.

3   Right click the selected navbar and choose **Edit Navigation Bar...** from the menu.

4   Ensure that **Theme Graphic (Vertical)** is still selected and use the scroll bars to search through the available sets.

We chose **Clean**.

Click **OK**.

5   With the object still selected, click the ⎍ T ⎍.

The **Theme Graphics Settings** dialog will appear. Here you can change the font, fill colour, over colour and text colour. We simply want to change the font.

6 Check **Specify a font for this Theme Graphic** and select a new font from the list. We chose **Cooper Black**.

Click **OK**.

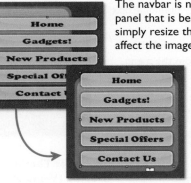

The navbar is now much too big for the grey panel that is below it. However, we can't simply resize the panel to fit as this would affect the images on the other site pages.

7 Drag the navbar so that the 'Contact Us' bar is aligned with the bottom of the grey panel. The navbar is still too wide so resize it by dragging the handles inwards.

8 The navbar is still a little long, so let's extend the panel upwards so that it fits. However, before we do that, right click the navbar, choose **Arrange>Lock Objects** so that we can't accidentally select it.

> Theme Graphics are always rasterized (exported as graphics) when the site is published. This means that you can choose any from font, even those that are not 'Web Safe'.

9   The grey panel is actually two objects. Drag a marquee around them both to select them. The  button will appear when you have both selected. Group the items and drag the handle upwards so that the navbar fits inside.

That's it! Preview the site in your browser to see the new navbar in action.

We've made some subtle changes to our site, but what if we want something more drastic? For example, suppose we want to totally change the colours used throughout the site.

Of course, we could select each element individually and then apply colours from the **Swatches** or **Colour** tab. This would take a lot of effort on our part, and we'd have to make a note of our original colours if we wanted to revert to the original design.

Fortunately, the designer of this template has used a WebPlus **colour scheme**, providing a quick and easy way to help us with this task.

To change the colour scheme of a site

1   Click outside the page area to deselect everything, and then on the Page Context toolbar click ◇ Colour Scheme .

2   In the **Scheme Manager** dialog, on the **Schemes** tab, the colour schemes are listed on the left. The currently selected scheme is highlighted—**Megabyte01**. Notice that the five colours displayed alongside the scheme name correspond to the five numbered swatches displayed on the **Swatches** tab.

3   Scroll through the various colour schemes and click on a few. In the right **Preview** pane, you'll see your Web page update with the new scheme colours.

4   When you've chosen the scheme you
prefer—we like **Megabyte02** but edited it
to have a black background and page
colour—click **OK** to apply it.

What else can you do to change this template?
The simple answer is "Lots!" It all depends on
the purpose of your site (and how adventurous
you are feeling!). Obviously, you can add more
pages; insert your own images and text;
edit existing hyperlinks and anchors and
add new ones. But why not take
advantage of some WebPlus X2
features, for example...

• Share those special photographs
with family and friends by creating a
photo gallery Web page—see
"WebPlus Projects: Creating a
Personal Web Site."

- or -

• Sign up for Serif Web Resources and add interactive or dynamic
Smart objects, such as hit counters, polls, blogs, and mailing lists—
see "WebPlus Projects: Adding Dynamic Content to Your Site."

- or -

• Add e-commerce functionality so you can sell your products
online—see "WebPlus Projects: Creating an E-Commerce Web
Site."

Whether you're just beginning to work with WebPlus, or an old hand
exploring new design possibilities, using a template speeds you through
the process of creating a professional site.

> 💡 You can edit the WebPlus colour
> schemes and even create your own from
> scratch. For details, see the "Getting
> Started: Working With Colour Schemes"
> tutorial.

2: The WebPlus Gallery

The **Gallery** tab provides you with a wide variety of predesigned, customizable elements that you can use as a starting point for, or add to, your own designs. In addition, the gallery also lets you store your own design objects (pictures, text blocks, HTML fragments, and so on) for use in future Web site layouts. Once you've copied a design to the gallery, it becomes available to any Web site from the **Gallery** tab.

In this section, we'll use gallery elements to build a site from scratch.

> The files used in this project are located in the the **Workspace** folder of your WebPlus installation directory.
>
> In a standard installation, this is installed to the following location:
>
> **C:\Program Files\Serif\WebPlus\X2\Tutorials\Workspace**
>
> If you want to take a look at the finished sample Web page (**FloTherapy.wpp**) you'll also find it in this folder.
>
>

1   Click the **Gallery** tab. (If you can't see this tab, click **View**, select **Studio tabs**, and then select **Gallery Tab**.)

2   At the top of the tab, click to expand the drop-down list and then expand the **Manual Web Graphics** category list.

    In the category list, click the **Metal Sheet** category.

3   In the lower section of the tab, thumbnails representing the designs in the **Metal Sheet** category are displayed.

    Drag the **Large Panel** element from the tab on to your page.

4   On the Tools toolbar, click **Import Picture**. In the **Import Picture** dialog, do the following:

  • Browse to your **Tutorials\Workspace** folder and select the **Sunflower.png** file.

  • In the right of the dialog, select the **Link picture** option.

  • Click **Open**.

5   Click on your page to insert the image at default size.

   Click and drag it into position in the upper left corner of the panel object.

6   On the Standard toolbar, click the button to place the image behind the panel.

Before we continue, let's choose a colour scheme for our site. We want to use colours that are appropriate for the 'image' of the site—something to convey a tranquil and calming mood.

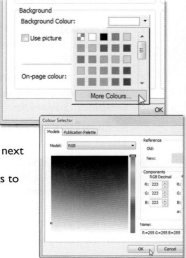

7   On the **Tools** menu, click **Scheme Manager**. On the **Schemes** tab, select the **Stones** colour scheme.

   On the **Edit** tab, click the down arrow next to background colour. Choose **More Colours...** and change the RGB settings to **223, 223, 223** on the **Models** tab.

   Click **OK** twice to apply the scheme.

Notice that the background page colour and panel border colour have both changed, but the flower is still yellow. We can change this by applying a scheme colour to our image.

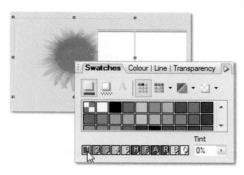

8 Select the sunflower image and then click the **Swatches** tab.

   At the bottom of the **Swatches** tab, click the **Scheme Colour I** swatch to apply it to the image.

> 💡 You can edit the WebPlus colour schemes or create your own from scratch.
>
> For step-by-step instructions, and advice about choosing the perfect colour scheme for your site, see the "Getting Started: Working With Colour Schemes" tutorial.

9 Repeat steps 4 and 5 to import and place the **Lily.png** image so that it overlaps the left and lower edges of the panel slightly, as illustrated.

10 With the image selected, click the **⊐ Square Crop** tool and then crop the left and lower edges so that the lily sits inside the panel.

   Let's now return to the **Gallery** tab and add some more elements to our page.

11 Expand the **Metal Sheet** category and drag the **Menu Vertical**
and **Small Panel** elements on to your page. Position these
elements as illustrated below.

We used Serif
PhotoPlus to remove the
background from our
original flower images and
create transparent PNG
files.

12 Import the **Couple.jpg** image and then use the ⌗ **Square Crop**
tool to crop away most of the image, leaving just the woman's face.

13 Click the ↖ **Pointer** tool and drag the image
into position inside the **Small Panel** element.

14 With the image still selected, click the
Swatches tab and then click the **Scheme
Colour 1** swatch to apply it.

15 On the **Gallery** tab, in the **Manual Web
Graphics** section, click the
Metal Sheet category.

Drag a **Bullet** element on
to the **Large Panel** already
on your page.

16 Select the bullet, click
Edit, and then click
Replicate.

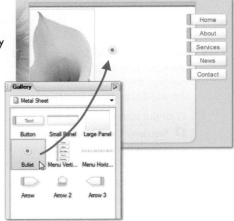

17 In the **Replicate** dialog:

- In the **Replicate Method** section, choose **Create Line**.

- In the **Replicate Count** section, enter a **Line Length** of **4**.

- In the **Spacing** section, select **Offset** and enter a **Horizontal** spacing of **0** and a **Vertical** spacing of **27** pixels.

- Click **OK**.

WebPlus creates a line of four evenly-spaced bullets.

18 Drag the line of bullets into position to the right of the lily, as illustrated.

Great, the main elements of our Web page are in place. All that remains is to add our logo and some text objects. We assume that you are already familiar with the various WebPlus text objects, so in the following section we'll summarize how we completed our layout rather than explaining the step-by-step procedures.

Creating the logo

Our clean and simple logo is comprised of three separate elements. Here's how we created it...

1 We created the letter 'f' with the **A Artistic Text** tool, choosing **43 pt Bold Arial** font.

2 For the circle surrounding the 'f,' we used the **Quick Donut** (located on the Standard Objects toolbar, on the QuickShapes flyout).

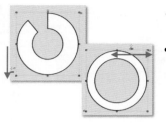

- We dragged the left node down to close the shape.

- We dragged the upper node to adjust the width until it matched the width of the letter 'f.'

3   We added a second artistic text frame for the company name 'flotherapy.'

This time we selected **20 pt Arial** font, applying **Bold** formatting to the first three letters only.

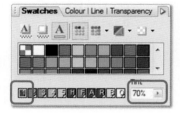

4   Finally, on the **Swatches** tab, we applied **Scheme Colour 1** to all of our logo elements, adjusting the value in the **Tint** box to 70%.

Creating the small panel text

We used another artistic text object for this.

1   For the words 'Natural therapeutic,' we used **21 pt Bold Times New Roman** font.

2   For the words 'services for all the family' we used **18 pt Regular Times New Roman** font.

3   We applied **Scheme Colour 1** with a 40% **Tint** value to all of the text.

Creating the large panel text

We used two artistic text objects.

1   For the first line, 'ask yourself,' we used **23.4 pt Bold Arial** font.

2   For the second line, 'talk to us now,' we used **32.2 pt Bold Arial** font.

3   For the third line we used **27.6 pt Regular Arial** font.

4   We applied **Scheme Colour 1** to
     all of the text, with the following
     Tint values:

     • 'ask'—60%

     • 'yourself'—50%

     • 'talk to us'—60%

     • 'now'—50%

     • 'on 0123 456 789'—70%

Creating the bullet point text

We used four  **Creative** text
frames.

1   We chose **9 pt Regular Arial** font.

2   We applied **Scheme Colour 1**
     with a Tint value of 0%.

3   We selected all of the text objects
     and clicked the ⌐ **Align Left**
     button on the **Align** tab.

Creating the copyright text

We used a **Creative** text frame.

1   We chose **7 pt Regular Arial** font.

2   We applied **Scheme Colour 1 with a Tint** value of 60%.

Copyright FloTherapy 2006. All Rights Reserved

That's all there is to it! We've created an effective, professional-looking page layout using predesigned gallery elements, which we've customized to fit the theme of our Web site.

What's more, because we've used a WebPlus colour scheme, we can quickly and easily change the look of our site by simply switching schemes.

Let's try this now.

To change colour schemes

1   Click **Tools**, then **Scheme Manager** (or click the **Colour Scheme** button on the Page context toolbar).

2   In the **Scheme Manager** dialog, on the **Schemes** tab, click on a few different schemes.

    Your page updates in the **Preview** pane.

3   When you're happy with the scheme you've chosen, click **OK** to apply it to your site.

That concludes this section of the project. We've given you just a taste of the possibilities provided by the WebPlus gallery, and hope we've inspired you to experiment further with these powerful tools.

> 💡 **In this exercise, w**e've worked with **Manual Web Graphics**, but don't forget to explore the other categories available on the **Gallery** tab.
>
> For information on adding and editing Flash banners, see the "Creating Personal Web Sites: Adding Flash Banners" tutorial.

3: Web Site examples

The following examples illustrate some of the possibilities provided by WebPlus, and give you some insight into the way in which professional Web designers construct Web page layouts. We hope that they'll also provide creative inspiration for your own design ideas.

Handheld Direct

The HandHeld Direct site uses graphics created entirely in WebPlus, themed graphics, and various other gallery objects.

The large blue panel with its overlaid white corner sections, was created using Quick Rectangles and Quick Buttons. The designer then applied various fills, outlines, transparency, and filter effects to the shapes (e.g., drop shadow) to achieve the final 'layered' effect.

The navbar was created from scratch, using QuickShapes (with various effects applied) layered on top of each other to give a glass effect.

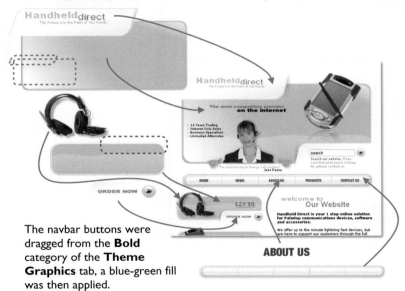

The navbar buttons were dragged from the **Bold** category of the **Theme Graphics** tab, a blue-green fill was then applied.

Also of note are the Contact Us page, which contains a Web Form (see "WebPlus Projects: Creating a Personal Web Site"), and the Products page, which uses predesigned flags from the **Gallery** tab.

mJames Photography

The mJames Photography site displays a photo gallery, a Web form, and a selection of Smart objects—hit counter, blog, poll, and shout box.

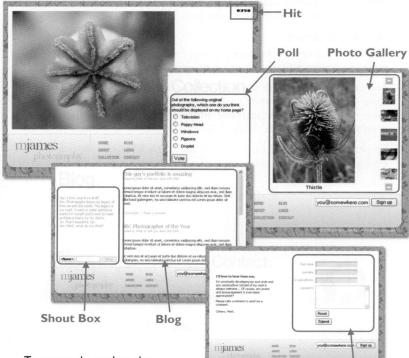

Hit

Poll

Photo Gallery

Shout Box

Blog

Web Form

To create the navbar, the designer used a Quick Rectangle, applying gradient fills and various other effects. The navbar buttons are theme graphics customized with a bright orange fill.

If you'd like to know exactly how the mJames Photography site was created, you'll find step-by-step instructions in the "Creating a Personal Web Site" and "Adding Dynamic Content to Your Site" WebPlus projects.

Lights On

The Lights On site demonstrates how you can construct an effective commercial Web site using a variety of easy-to-use WebPlus features.

The site banner and main panels were constructed from scratch using QuickShapes, to which transparency effects were applied.

The site's main navigation elements and headings were taken directly from the **Theme Graphics** tab (the **Ahead** set).

The Photo Gallery and Products pages illustrate two very different WebPlus photo gallery layouts.

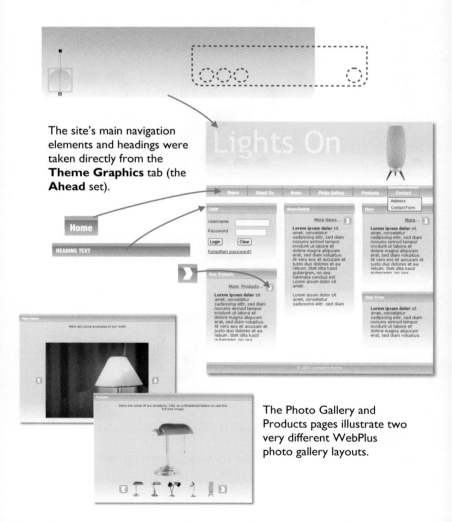

Sharon's Blog

This personal site uses a
clean and simple layout. All
design and navigation
elements were taken from
the **Gallery** tab. To complete the
site, the designer included a photo
gallery and some Smart objects.

A project like this provides a great opportunity to work with a wide
range of WebPlus
features, without
getting involved in
complex site
structure and page
layouts.

Photo Gallery

Blog

Hit
Counter

That concludes this project.
We hope you've found it
interesting, and have picked
up a few tips along the way.
We've introduced you to the
various ways you can create a
Web site. We hope you're
feeling more comfortable

Shout Box

with the tools we've illustrated and are feeling inspired to start
constructing your own sites.

Working With Colour Schemes

When designing your Web site, one of the most important factors to consider is colour. Choose wisely and you'll attract the attention of your target audience, set the appropriate mood, and send the right message. Choose unwisely and you'll turn viewers away—no matter how professional your layout or how interesting your content.

But how do you select a colour palette that's right for your site? In this tutorial, we'll demystify the process and show you a few different ways to choose a colour scheme for your projects. You'll learn how to:

- Apply a preset colour scheme from the Scheme Manager.
- Modify an existing colour scheme.
- Create your own colour scheme from scratch.
- Create a colour scheme from a photograph.
- Use colour theory to create a range of palettes.

Working With Colour Schemes

In the first section of this tutorial, we'll apply scheme colours to individual elements on a site. We'll then show you how you can edit and modify scheme colours. Finally, we'll create a custom colour scheme from scratch.

Applying scheme colours to objects

You can apply a colour scheme at any point during the design process. Each publication can have just one colour scheme at a time and can easily switch from one to another.

Site Structure   Site Manager   Colour Scheme   Layout Guides   Resize Pages   Set User Details   Options   Page Security

To apply a colour scheme

1 From the WebPlus Startup Wizard, select **Create > Use Design Template** and select a template of your choice. Click **Open**.

2 On the Page context toolbar, click **Colour Scheme** (or click **Tools**, then **Scheme Manager**).

   In the **Scheme Manager** dialog, click the **Schemes** tab.

   You'll see an assortment of named schemes, each consisting of five basic colours. The colour scheme that is currently applied throughout this site is highlighted.

3 Click a few different colour schemes.

   As you select each new scheme, watch the **Preview** pane—you'll see various elements on the page (including theme graphics and the page background) change colour.

So what exactly is happening here?

The scheme colours work like a paint-by-numbers system, where regions and elements of a page are coded with numbers. In each scheme, a specific colour is assigned to each number.

> 🕛 When you save a site, its current colour scheme is saved with the project file.

When you switch to a different scheme, any elements that have been assigned one of the scheme colour numbers are updated with the corresponding colour from the new scheme. Let's see this in action...

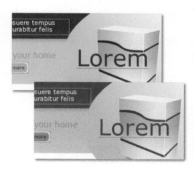

4 On the Tools toolbar, click the **A Artistic Text** tool and create a large text object on your page.

5 Click **Tools**, then **Scheme Manager** and switch to a different colour scheme.

Notice that the colour of your new text object changes.

Let's try the same experiment with a QuickShape.

6 On the Tools toolbar, click the ☐ **Quick Rectangle** and draw a shape on your page.

7 Open the **Scheme Manager** and switch to a different scheme. This time, the object does not update with the new scheme colours.

8 Click to display the **Swatches** tab. At the bottom of the tab, the five basic colours in the current colour scheme appear as numbered swatches.

The colours for **Hyperlink**, **Followed Hyperlink**, **Active Hyperlink**, **Rollover Hyperlink**, **Background** and **On-page colour** display with the labels H, F, A, R, B and O.

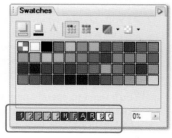

9 Select your shape, then on the
   Swatches tab:

   • Click the 🔲 **Fill** button and then
     click the scheme colour you want
     to apply.

   • Click the 🔲 **Line** button and
     then apply a different scheme
     colour to the shape's outline.

   Now let's see what happens when
   we switch colour schemes...

10 Click **Tools**, then **Scheme Manager**, and choose a different
   colour scheme.

   In the WebPlus workspace, your shape is updated with the new
   scheme colour.

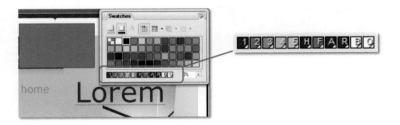

   Notice too that the colour scheme swatches at the bottom of the
   Swatches tab have also been replaced with the new colours.

   As you can see, when you create new elements in a Web template
   site, or start a site from scratch, you
   can extend a colour scheme to the
   new objects using the process just
   described.

   You'll need to spend some time
   working out which colour
   combinations look best, but the
   mechanics of the process are simple.

   > 💧 If you copy an object
   > that uses scheme colours to
   > another site, the object will
   > take on the new site's
   > colour scheme.

Modifying colour schemes

If you've tried various colour schemes but haven't found one that's quite right for your site, you can modify any of the colours in an existing scheme to create a new one.

To modify a colour scheme

1   On the Page Context bar, click **Colour Scheme**.

2   On the **Schemes** tab, select any colour scheme.

3   On the **Edit** tab, the current scheme colours are displayed.

Each of the five scheme colour numbers (plus the **Hyperlink**, **Followed Hyperlink**, **Active Hyperlink**, **Rollover Hyperlink**, **Background** and **On-page Colour**) has its own drop-down list, showing available colours in the WebPlus palette.

4   To set or change a scheme colour, click to expand the drop-down list, and then select a new colour.

5   **Optional:** If the drop-down palette doesn't contain the colour you want to use, click **More Colours** to display the **Colour Selector**.

In the **Colour Selector**
dialog, you can choose a
colour to apply or mix your
own custom colours.

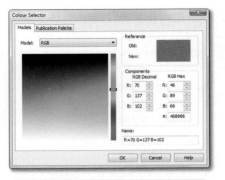

- The **Models** tab
  displays the colour
  space of the currently
  selected colour model.

- The **Publication
  Palette** tab lets you
  modify the set of
  colours associated with
  the current site.

6 When you have modified
   your scheme on the **Edit**
   tab, save it by clicking
   Save Scheme.

   💡 You can extend the Colour
   Selector's **Publication Palette** tab using
   the **Palette Manager**, which lets you
   modify the site's current palette and also
   load and save named palettes.

   For more information, see "Managing
   Colours and Palettes" in online Help.

   - If you are modifying an
     existing scheme, leave
     the name unchanged
     and click **OK**.

   - If you are creating a new scheme,
     type in a new name and click **OK**.

7 If you have saved your changes with a
   new name click the **Schemes** tab
   and then scroll the list to locate the
   new colour scheme.

⚬ The **Save Scheme** and **OK** buttons yield different results.

Each site stores a locally defined scheme, which may or may not correspond to a named scheme.

Modifying a scheme in the **Scheme Manager** and then clicking **Save Scheme** updates the named scheme, but *does not* apply it to the publication.

To ensure the publication uses the latest copy of the named scheme, click **OK** in the **Scheme Manager** or reapply the named scheme using the **Scheme Manager**.

When modifying a scheme repeatedly, make sure your site is using the latest version.

Creating custom colour schemes

There may be times when you want to create a new colour scheme from scratch, perhaps using colours from your company logo or an image on your Web site.

To complete this section, you can use our sample photograph or any image of your choice. You'll find the sample photograph, **Cocktail.jpg**, in the **Workspace** folder of your WebPlus installation directory. In a standard installation, this folder is copied to the following location:

C:\Program Files\Serif\WebPlus\X2\Tutorials\Workspace.

To create a custom colour scheme from an image

1   On the **Tools** toolbar, click 🖼 **Import Picture** and browse to locate the image you want to use.

Click **Open**, and then click and drag to place the image on your page.

2   Select the image and then on the Picture context toolbar, click 🖉 Image Adjustments (or right-click the image and choose **Image Adjustments**).

3 In the **Image Adjustments** dialog, click **Add Adjustment** and then select **Median**.

The **Median** adjustment panel, containing a **Radius** slider, is added to the dialog.

4 Drag the slider to the right so that colours making up the image blend into colour 'blocks,' as illustrated below. Click **OK**.

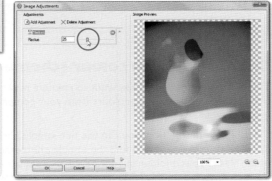

The Median filter is normally used to reduce 'noise' in an image.

5 Back in the WebPlus workspace, on the Tools toolbar, select the ▭ ▾ **Quick Rectangle** and draw a small square on your page (ours was about 60 x 60 pixels).

6 Select the shape, hold down the **Ctrl** key, and then drag to the right to create a copy.

7 Repeat the previous step to create five identical squares.

8 Select the first square, click the **Colour** tab, and then click the 🖋 **Colour Picker**.

9 On the image, click and drag to select the first colour you want to add to your new colour scheme.

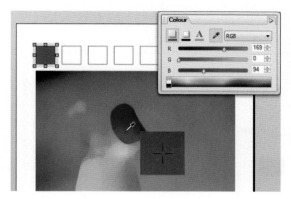

The popup colour sample updates as you drag to different areas of the image.

When you are happy with the colour displayed in the sample, release the mouse button.

The selected colour is applied to the square and added to the **Swatches** tab.

10 Selecting each of the remaining squares in turn, repeat the previous step to fill the shapes with four additional colours from your image.

11 On the **Swatches** tab, scroll to the end of the palette swatches to find your new custom colours displayed.

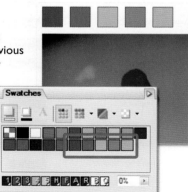

We're now ready to create our new colour scheme.

💡 You don't have to use QuickShapes to display your selected colours, but we think it's useful to see the colour swatches next to each other and the image on the page.

This allows you to determine if the colours work together with the image, and when isolated from the image. You can quickly and easily adjust the colours, pick new ones, or change the colour order, before deciding on your final scheme colours.

We used five squares—one for each main scheme colour—but you can create more than this to begin with. Once you've filled your squares with a selection of colours you can then decide on your final palette.

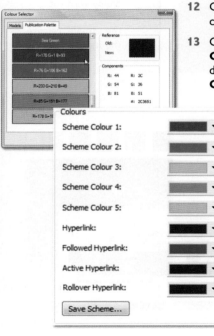

12 Open the **Scheme Manager** and click the **Edit** tab.

13 Click the arrow next to **Scheme Colour 1** to expand the drop-down palette, then click **More Colours**.

In the **Colour Selector** dialog, click the **Publication Palette** tab and scroll to the end of the palette list to find your custom colours.

14 Click the colour you want to assign to Scheme Colour 1 and click **OK**.

15 Repeat the previous step to assign the remaining scheme colours.

16 Click **Save Scheme** and type a name for your colour scheme.

17 On the **Schemes** tab, scroll to find your new colour scheme.

18 Click the **Swatches** tab. Note that the swatches at the bottom of the tab now display your custom scheme colours.

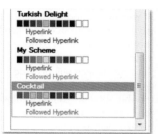

You can use these swatches to apply scheme colours to objects on your Web pages.

Congratulations, you've created a custom colour scheme from scratch! It's a relatively simple process, but one which we hope you'll find useful in your future Web site designs.

We'll conclude this tutorial with a brief discussion about colour in general. While the use of colour is quite personal, our aim is to help you choose colours that are not only visually pleasing but also reflect the content your Web site presents.

Note that colour schemes are saved globally, so you'll be able to apply this scheme to your future WebPlus publications.

Choosing colours

Designers use many different methods of choosing colours for their Web sites. In this example, we based our colour scheme on an image that we wanted to use on the Master page of our site. As mentioned previously, you might also take colours from a company logo or some other 'signature' image.

Alternatively, you could use an image that does not appear on the site, but which contains a range of colours you find particularly attractive and which portrays the mood and message you want your site to convey to your audience.

If you want a more structured approach, you can even employ a little basic colour theory! A quick Internet search will provide you with lots of information on this subject—try searching on "use of colour in Web design" for example.

> 🛈 Don't underestimate the importance of colour choice when designing your Web site.
>
> No matter how professional your layout or how interesting your content, incorrect use of colour can result in pages that are ugly and/or difficult to read.

In this section, we'll step you through the following approaches:

- **Example 1:** Find an image or photograph that portrays the mood or message of the site—this may not necessarily be related to the site's content—then choose a range of colours from the image.

- **Example 2:** Choose a 'base' colour (you can take this from an image that will feature on your site), then use colour theory to find colours that harmonize with it.

Example 1: Using an image or photograph

Suppose we're creating a Web site for a health spa. The first thing we need to do is think about the image we want to portray. We associate health spas with calmness and tranquility—it makes sense, therefore, not to use harsh or vibrant colours on our site.

1 Choose a few images that suit the mood of the site. You could use a photograph, or an image found on the Internet or in a book or magazine (you'll need to scan the image so that you can open it on your computer).

The colour palettes of our sample photographs all reflect the mood we want our health spa site to convey.

Looking at these images, it's obvious that they fall into two distinct groups: one group contains various shades of blue along with natural and more muted tones; in the other group, softer earth tones predominate.

2　At this point, you (or your client) must decide which colour palette to use. For this tutorial, we'll assume that our health spa client prefers the muted tones of the 'pebbles' close-up photo.

3　You can now follow the procedure outlined previously to create your custom colour scheme (see "Creating custom colour schemes from scratch").

We suggest you start by creating lots of squares and fill them with a range of colours from the image.

When you have a good selection from which to choose, play around with the swatches and try different groupings before settling on your final five scheme colours.

4　If the choice is not obvious to you, create several different schemes using variations of your colour swatches. You can then switch between schemes to see how the look and feel of the site changes.

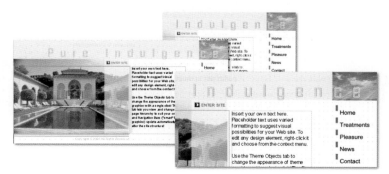

Example 2: Using colour theory

This method starts with the selection of a 'base' colour. You can choose any colour you prefer.

In our example, we'll take our base colour from a photograph that will feature on the Web site of a fictitious holiday company.

1 Follow the procedure outlined previously to extract a wide range of colours from your image (see "Creating custom colour schemes from scratch").

   - Don't forget to add the **Median** image adjustment first, to create blocks of colour to work with.

   - Start with the 'big' colours. These are the ones you see first when you glance at the image: skin, hair, and shirt. Then extract the 'small' colours—mouth, eyes, highlights and shadows.

   - You need a good range of colours, but don't overdo it or you'll find it difficult to make your selection. You might only extract eight or ten colours, or you might find you need more. The exact number will vary depending on your image.

The WebPlus colour schemes are designed with colours arranged from left to right, darkest to lightest, starting with Scheme Colour 1. The templates, theme objects, and samples are designed with this in mind so you'll notice that backgrounds are generally assigned the lightest of the scheme colours.

When creating your schemes, you'll get the best results if you follow this standard:

1 Start with the darkest colour and assign it to Scheme Colour 1.

2 Choose the next darkest colour for Scheme Colour 2.

3 Continue like this until you finish by assigning the lightest colour to Scheme Colour 5, or to the Background colour if you are using this.

2   Group your results by colour, then sort each colour group by value from dark to light, deleting any colours that are too similar.

3   Select any one of your colours as your 'base colour.' Locate the colour on the colour wheel to determine whether it is warm or cool, and to see its relationship to other colours.

  • Our **warm colours** are found in the red areas of girl's shirt, and in her hair and skin tones. Choose from these colours if your aim is to give a softer, gentler look and feel to your site.

  • Our **cool colours** are derived from the blue and white areas of the shirt, and from the eyes. These colours are generally used when a more serious or business-like approach is required.

4   Using your base colour and its position on the colour wheel, you can now start to create a range of colour palettes. There are several approaches you can take, including:

  • Analogous

  • Monochromatic

  • Complement

  • Split complement

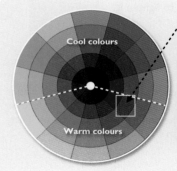

The Colour Wheel

The colour wheel is a basic model. It is meant as a guide only, so don't worry if you can't find an exact match for your colour.

Once you've located your base colour you can see its relationship to other colours and can then create a range of colour palettes that will work for your Web site.

Analogous colour palettes

Analogous colours are extracted from the two sections that sit either side of the base colour section. These colours all share the same undertone—in our example, red-orange, red, and red-purple.

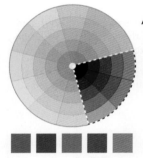

Analogous colour combinations are great for Web design as they are harmonious and very easy to work with.

Monochromatic colour palettes

Monochromatic palettes consist of the dark, medium, and light values (the shades and tints) of your base colour.

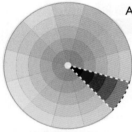

A **shade** is made by adding black to a colour to darken it.

A **tint** is made by adding white to a colour to lighten it.

(You can choose your colour swatch values from the WebPlus palette, and then further increase the contrast by adjusting the **Tint** controls on the **Colour** tab.)

Complement colour palettes

You'll find the complement colours directly opposite the base colour range. Generally, the complement (in our case, the green range) is used as an accent. These palettes provide extreme contrast, conveying energy and excitement.

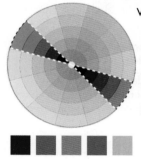

While often used in printed media, you should be wary of using this palette in Web design as such highly contrasted colours tend to be jarring to the eye when viewed on screen.

Split complement colour palettes

The split complement colours are the analogous colours of the complement itself.

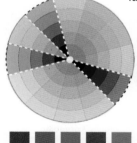

Less jarring than the complement, this combination provides a more subtle contrast and a more harmonious palette.

In this example, the base colour red would be used as the accent colour in our design layout.

Mixing palettes

If you're feeling adventurous, you can also combine palettes to create some interesting effects.

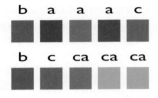

For example, try contrasting your **base colour and its analogous colours** with the **complement**.

Alternatively, you could combine your **base colour and its complement** with the **complement's analogous colours**.

As you can see from our illustrations, each palette creates quite a different effect when applied to the same layout. Which one you choose depends on the message you want your site to convey to your viewers.

Accessibility

When choosing your colour schemes, it is worth bearing in mind that a small percentage of the population are colour blind and cannot differentiate between certain colours (the most common being red and green). To illustrate this, here are a few examples of the colour wheel when viewed by someone with one of the three main forms of colour blindness, protanope, deuteranope, and the rare tritanope:

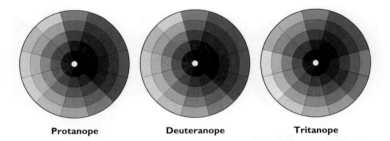

Protanope   **Deuteranope**   **Tritanope**

There is an excellent Web site called Vischeck that explains colour blindness in more detail. It also has a free plugin available for download that allows you to test your own site for colour use. The plugin works with Serif PhotoPlus and was used to create the images found within this tutorial.

Visit the site at http://www.vischeck.com/

The following sample image serves well to illustrate the care needed when deciding on colour schemes. This example simulates deuteranope colour blindness, as this is the most common form of the three. Notice how the browns and the reds appear almost identical.

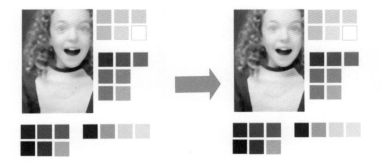

That concludes our tutorial. We've covered a lot of material here; we hope you've enjoyed working through the exercises and have learned something along the way. You should now be feeling comfortable creating your own colour schemes from scratch, and understand a little more about effective use of colour in Web design.

Have fun experimenting!

Creating Web-Friendly Sites

This tutorial presents useful tips and tricks to help you achieve a more Web-friendly design and make your sites more efficient.

The following topics are discussed:

- How Z-order and cropping and rotating of text objects affect the way in which text is published.

- How applying transparency, fills, warps, and various filter effects can alter the way in which text is published.

- Non-Web fonts, Websafe fonts, and HTML frames.

- Alignment options.

- Image thumbnails, hotspots, and image maps.

1: Publishing text

While you can perform all manner of design tweaks to text, the following tips will make you aware of which design features cause text to be published as a graphic instead of as simple text. There is no harm in some text being converted to a graphic when your site is published, but if this is the case for a large number of text objects it will more notably affect your site's download speed.

1   Start a new, blank site.

2   On the Standard Objects toolbar, on the QuickShapes flyout, click the ☐ **Quick Rectangle** and then draw and fill two rectangles, overlapping them slightly.

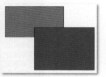

Notice that the second shape you created sits on top of the first one. This demonstrates a concept called '**Z-order**.'

In dimension terms, X and Y are indicators of horizontal and vertical position. The Z-plane or dimension is most commonly encountered in 3D charts or 3D design. So, how can a 2D Web page (or printed page for that matter) have a third dimension?

Each time you create an object on the page in WebPlus, it has a position in a 'virtual stack,' and has a **stack height**. In our example, the second rectangle is 'higher' in the stack than the other—it sits on top of the stack and obscures what is behind it. Stack height and Z-order are identical; of the two objects, the one on top is higher in the Z-order.

Z-order

Try and keep your text objects highest in the Z-order, that is, keep text at the top or front of your design layering. If any objects—for example, partially transparent shapes—are on top of your text they will cause the text to be published as a graphic.

To move an object forward or backward through the Z-order:

* Select the object and then, on the Arrange toolbar, click ⬜ **Forward One** or ⬜ **Back One**.

WebPlus always attempts to faithfully reproduce your design as an HTML Web page, which means converting some 'tweaked' text to graphics to maintain their look—HTML code alone can't always reproduce your design.

If you keep text at the front of the Z-order with no overlapping objects or effects, it should be published as text, which is very quick to download.

Some design features aren't directly replicable using the language of the Web, HTML. Again, this can notably affect text and cause it to be published as an image, meaning your page will take longer to download. (The images may not necessarily be too large or too slow to download, but they will be slower than plain text!) This doesn't mean you can't use such design features, but you should be aware that there are some consequences regarding download efficiency.

Cropping and rotating

If you use the ⊐ **Square Crop** or ⟳ **Rotate** tools to manipulate your objects they will be published as graphics in order to accurately recreate your design as a Web site. This is because there's no equivalent of a crop or rotate command in the language of the Web, HTML.

Fancy fills and transparency

Similarly, HTML alone cannot reproduce fancy fills or transparency. Try to use solid fills on your text objects rather than gradient or bitmap fills, which force the text to be published as a graphic.

You can sometimes enhance the look of objects with transparency, and create some impressive artistic effects, but text cannot remain as pure text when publishing if such effects are used.

Mesh warping

Located on the Effects flyout, the **Warp** tool can be used to produce some great effects, but when used on text it will cause it to be published as a graphic.

Using this or other effects on drawn or imported artwork won't be harmful, as non-text objects are published as graphics regardless of any fills, transparency, or effects. Generally speaking, the more complicated the look of an object, the larger its resultant graphic file size.

Filter effects and Instant 3D

Some filter effects, such as drop shadow, allow the text to be published as plain text with a small graphic behind it as the shadow, but most filter effects (and Instant 3D) modify the text to such an extent that the whole object is published as an image.

Non-Web fonts

HTML and the browsers that interpret it to display Web pages will accurately display your design only if the fonts you have used for your text exist on your site visitors' computers too.

However, you may design a headline in a beautiful script font, or modern 'fun' font, and it will look perfect when you preview your site because you already have that font installed. Unfortunately, a user viewing your published site might not have the same font installed. In this case, an alternate font is used. You have no control over this substitution, and it may well spoil the look of your page.

To counteract this effect, you can do one of the following:

- Use Websafe fonts. In WebPlus, Websafe fonts are listed by default in the left **Fonts** tab, and are denoted with a check mark in the context toolbar's Fonts drop-down list.

- Convert text objects that use fancy fonts into graphics before you publish.

- For frame text, use the ▦ **HTML Frame** tool (discussed below) instead of the ▣ **Creative Frame** tool. This will ensure that any text in the frames is HTML-compliant and will remain as text when your site is published.

HTML frame text

If it's important to minimize the amount of time it takes your viewers to access the information on your Web site, you should use HTML text frames. The main advantages of HTML text are as follows:

- Text contained in HTML frames is always published as text and is never converted to a graphic.

- HTML frames are searchable by Web search engines such as Google™.

- HTML frames let you design with HTML-compliant styles, which means that you can format text in your HTML frame using heading styles from H1, H2, ..., to H6. Text applied with these 'Heading' styles is given priority in Internet search engines.

> 💡 How do you tell the difference between an HTML and a Creative text frame?
>
> When selected, HTML frames have dark blue corner/edge handles, while a Creative frame's handles are grey.
>
> See "Understanding text frames" in online Help.

For more information, see the "Getting Started: Working With Text," and "Creating Business Web Sites: Optimizing Your Site for Search Engines" tutorials.

2: Aligning Objects

When designing the layout of your site and positioning objects on the page, you should pay attention to object alignment.

If your site is very informally laid out, you can take a more relaxed approach, but the neatness of aligned elements makes the information you are offering easier to digest.

Aligning objects

With WebPlus, it's quick and easy to align objects using the **Align** tab.

1 On the **Theme Objects** tab, browse one of the available theme sets and drag four Bullet elements onto your page. Select them all by dragging your mouse cursor diagonally to create a selection bounding box that encompasses all the bullets.

2 On the **Align** tab, click **Left** and **Space Evenly Down**.

   (You can also select the **Spaced** check box and use the adjacent box to set a point size by which objects are to be spaced.)

   Your bullets are left-aligned and evenly spaced.

> While WebPlus offers various methods to help you achieve a neat layout—for example, Layout Guides, Snapping, a Dot Grid, and Guide Lines—the **Align** tab (and **Align** dialog) have the added advantage of being able to evenly space objects and align them with each other or the page at the same time.

3: Importing Images

If you've worked through the "Getting Started: Importing Images" tutorial, you'll already know something about download efficiency and picture quality of graphics displayed on your Web site. This section reiterates some of the material covered there, and offers additional tips.

1 Click **Import Picture**, then browse to the **Workspace** folder of your WebPlus installation. In a default installation, you'll find this in the following location:

   C:\Program Files\Serif\WebPlus\X2\Tutorials\Workspace

2 Select the **SuzukiGSX-R98.png** file and open it.

This image is quite large (736 pixels wide on our 750 pixel-wide page). Need to know the most popular way of offering large images without ruining anyone's enjoyment of your site? Read on!

Thumbnail images

If you have lots of images to display on your site as part of its content, you might want to consider using thumbnails—small versions of your images. These will be speedy to download.

But what should you do if you still want people to access full-size images at their discretion? Here's a simple solution...

1 Click the image to select it and then resize it so that it is a fraction of its original size.

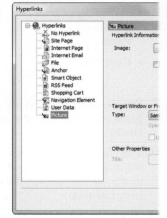

2 On the Tools toolbar, on the Hyperlink flyout, click **Hyperlink** . In the **Hyperlinks** dialog, choose the **Picture** option and click **OK**.

3 Preview your site to examine the results of this change—the thumbnail image is tiny so downloads very quickly; when you click on it you can view the full-size original image.

If you have lots of pictures on offer this technique is much more efficient as it allows your site's visitors to download the page of images quickly, and then specifically choose which ones to examine at full size.

Close your preview and return to WebPlus.

4 On the **Site** tab, click ⊞ to add a second page. In the **Insert** dialog, accept the default page settings and click **OK**.

5 Return to the page containing your image. Increase the size of the image—by dragging a corner handle—until it is approximately half the width of your page.

6 Click  **Hyperlink**. In the **Hyperlinks** dialog, choose the **No Hyperlink** option and click **OK**.

7 On the Web Objects toolbar, click ▦ **Insert Hotspot**.

8 Draw a square approximately the same size as the motorbike's rear wheel.

- In the **Hyperlinks** dialog:

- Click the **Site Page** option.

- In the **Page name** drop-down list, choose **Page 2**.

- Click **OK**.

9 Double-click a point on the green square hotspot, clicking on the green line rather than the object's border.

10 This creates an additional 'node' on the shape. Click and drag the node to the nearest point on the wheel's circumference.

11 Repeat this process to create more nodes, dragging them into position around the wheel.

12 Preview your site and click on the wheel to see your hotspot in action.

You should jump to Page 2 of your site, which is blank for now.

Suppose our Page 2 contained information about motorbike wheels, for example. We could add more pages and hotspots for other bike parts. Our image with multiple hotspots linking to different pages would then be an **image map**.

Image maps

Use hotspots over parts of an image if you wish to link to different pages using an image map. For example, you can use a world map and make different continents link to different pages, or you can (as we have done in this tutorial) pick out components in a picture of your hobby subject or items that you sell through a business.

Image maps offer a different approach to page navigation and aren't likely to entirely replace navbars in your site, but they can be a fun and easy way for visitors to find what they're looking for.

That concludes this tutorial. We hope you've found these tips useful and will keep them in mind when designing and laying out your Web sites.

Creating Personal Web Sites

We assume that by now you're familiar with the basic tools and are ready to focus on how to get the best out of them.

The emphasis here is on combining various approaches to achieve impressive results, and tackling some of the more common personal Web site design scenarios.

- Creating a Personal Web Site
- Adding Dynamic Content to Your Site
- Adding Flash Objects to Your Site
- Adding a Flash Photo Gallery

Creating a Personal Web Site

In this project, we'll step you through the process of creating a personal Web site from scratch. Along the way, we'll point out some useful design and layout tips.

To complete this tutorial, you'll need a selection of photographs to add to your photo gallery.

In this exercise, we'll show you how to:

- Set up a master page.
- Set up site structure and navigation.
- Work with text objects.
- Add elements from the Theme Graphics tab.
- Create a photo gallery using popup rollovers.
- Create a simple Web-based email form

Creating a Personal Web Site

In this project, we'll create a personal Web site from scratch. The site will serve as a showcase for a photographer's work. Layout and structure is important as we want the site to be clean and simple, giving focus to the images.

We'll use some new WebPlus X2 functionality, using popup rollovers to create a 'photo gallery' from a selection of photographs. We'll also include some text objects and a Web form that visitors can use to send email to the photographer.

The sample photo images used in this tutorial are provided in your ...**Workspace\mjames** folder. In a standard installation, this folder is installed to the following location:

C:\Program Files\Serif\WebPlus\X2\Tutorials\Workspace

Setting up site structure and the master page

1 In the Startup Wizard, click **Start New Site**, or from WebPlus click **File** then **New**.

2 On the **Site** tab, in the ⊞ ▾ **Add** drop-down list, click **New Blank Page**. In the **Insert** dialog, click **OK**. You'll now see two pages displayed on the tab—'Home' and 'Page 2.' Right-click Page 2 and select **Page Properties**.

3 In the **Page Properties** dialog:

- In the **Page name:** text box, delete the default text and type 'About.'

- Select the **Specify HTML title** option and type 'About mJames.'

- Click the **Change...** button and in the **Web Page Properties** dialog change the page name to **about.html** and click **OK**.

- Click **OK**.

4 Repeat steps 2 and 3 to add four more pages.

Name the new pages 'Collection,' 'Equipment,' 'Links,' and 'Contact,' and change the HTML title and file names accordingly.

Our site pages are in place. Let's now set up our master page elements—the elements we want to display on every page of the site.

5 In the lower left corner of the workspace, click the arrow to expand the Page Manager and then click **Master A** to display the master page in the workspace.

6 On the Standard Objects toolbar, on the QuickShapes flyout, click the **Quick Rectangle** and draw a large rectangle, approximately 620 pixels wide by 420 pixels high, in the upper section of the page. (On the **Transform** tab, the **W** and **H** values display the exact width and height of your shape.)

7 Drag the left node down to round the corners.

8 With the shape selected, on the **Tools** menu, click **Convert to Curves**. Additional nodes appear around the border of the shape.

9 Click to select the upper left node, then press **Delete**. Repeat to delete the upper right node, creating square corners at the top of the shape.

> You can convert any shape or artistic text object to curves (editable lines and nodes). However, the new object—now a collection of line segments—will no longer possess its former properties. For example, you can't change the font of text that's been converted to curves.

10 With the rectangle selected, right-click and select **Copy**. Right-click again and select **Paste**.

11 With the new shape selected, click to select the upper left node, then hold down the **Shift** key and click the upper right node. Both nodes are now selected.

Release the **Shift** key, drag the nodes down until the shape is approximately 90 pixels high, and then drag it into position directly on top of the large shape.

12 Select both the shapes and then on the **Align** tab:

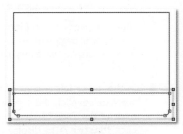

- Ensure that the **Include Margins** check box is cleared and then click the **Bottom** button.

- Select the **Include Margins** check box and then click the **Centre Horizontally** button.

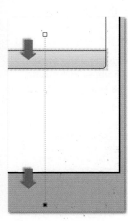

13 Select the small shape, and then on the Standard Objects toolbar click the ◇ **Fill** tool.

Draw a vertical line through the middle of the shape and then drag the top and bottom nodes down to create a subtle grey shading effect, as illustrated. Select the ▶ **Pointer** tool and set the line colour to 'none' on the **Line** tab.

Well done, you've just created a navbar from scratch!

To complete the effect, we'll add a drop shadow to both of our rectangle shapes.

14 Select the large rectangle and use the **Line** tab to set the line style
to 'none'. With the object still selected, click **Format**, and then
Filter Effects. In the **Filter Effects** dialog, select the following
options.

For the large rectangle:

- **Effect:** Drop Shadow
- **Opacity: 30**
- **Blur:** 2
- **Lock:** Centre
- **Distance:** 2
- **Angle:** 135

Use the following settings to apply
the drop shadow to the smaller
rectangle (navbar):

- **Effect:** Drop Shadow
- **Opacity: 30**
- **Blur:** I
- **Lock:** Centre
- **Distance:** I
- **Angle:** 270

We'll now create a subtle navbar 'divider' using two QuickShapes.

15 Click the ☐ **Quick Rectangle** and
create a long thin rectangle
anywhere on your page. On the
Transform tab, set the width of
the shape to 1 pixel and set the
height to two pixels less than the
height of your small rectangle.

Click the ⊕ **Zoom In** tool and
zoom in on your shape.

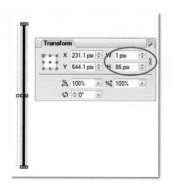

16 Create a copy of the shape and position it next to the original.

17 Select the leftmost shape and then on the **Swatches** tab, apply a light-grey fill and line—we used RGB (192, 192, 192).

18 Select the other shape and apply a white fill and line.

19 Select both lines and then on the **Align** tab, click ▣ **Centre Vertically**.

20 With the shapes still selected, click the ▣ **Group** button. Now drag the group into position on top of the small rectangle, at about the 200 pixel mark (approximately one third of the width of the rectangle).

The main layout of our master page is complete. All that remains is to add the title of our site, hyperlinks to the various pages, and a background. Let's start with the hyperlinks.

Adding hyperlinks, title, and background to the master page

1 Click the **Theme Graphics** tab. At the top of the tab, expand the **Types** category and then click **Button**. Scroll the thumbnails to locate the **Micro** 'BUTTON' style and drag it on to the page.

2 Select the button object and then click the ⬚Ｔ **Theme Graphics Edit** button.

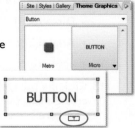

3 In the **Theme Graphics Settings** dialog:

- On the **Text** tab, select the **Specify text for this Theme Graphic** check box and then type 'HOME.'

- On the **Font** tab, select the **Specify a font for this Theme Graphic** check box and use the drop-down list to select a font style.

- On the **Text Colour** tab, select the **Specify a fill for this Theme Graphic** check box and click **Edit**.

  In the **Fill** dialog, select the fill colour for your button—we chose a vibrant orange, RGB (255, 128, 0)—and click **OK**.

- On the **Text Over Colour** tab, repeat the previous step to select the colour you want to apply to your button when the viewer hovers the cursor over it. We chose a lighter orange— RGB (255, 172, 0). Click **OK**.

- Click **OK** to close the dialog.

Great, we've created our **Home** page button. Now we can use it as a template for the other site page buttons.

4 Select the button and then use **Copy** (**Ctrl+C**) and **Paste** (**Ctrl+V**) to create five more buttons.

5 Selecting each button object in turn, repeat steps 2 and 3 to open the **Theme Graphics Settings** dialog and set the text of the buttons to correspond with the page titles listed on the **Site** tab.

6 Position the buttons as illustrated, using the **Align** tab to ensure precise alignment on the navbar.

Now let's add hyperlinks to our pages...

7 Right-click the Home button object and select **Hyperlink**.

In the **Hyperlinks** dialog, click the **Site Page** option and then in the **Page name** drop-down list, select the **Home** page.

Click **OK**.

8 Selecting each button in turn, repeat step 7 to add hyperlinks to the other pages of the site.

9 Preview the site in your browser to confirm that the navbar buttons are now linked to your Web site pages.

Now let's add a title and background to the site.

10 Use the **A Artistic Text** tool to create a title for your Web site. We used two separate artistic text objects, one for 'mjames,' and one for 'photography.'

11 Use the Text context toolbar to format the text as desired. You can use any font style and size you prefer. We used 30 pt Times New Roman for the first line; 20 pt Times New Roman for the second line.

12 Use the **Swatches** or **Colour** tab to choose the colour for your title, and adjust the **Tint** values if required.

For example, we used a grey fill—RGB (238, 238, 238) for all of our text and adjusted the **Tint** value as follows:

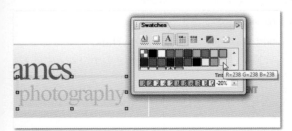

- 'm': -33%

- 'james': -57%

- 'photography': -20%

To complete our master page, we just need to set the background. We're going to use an image for this.

13 On the Page Context toolbar, click **Colour Scheme**, or (**Tools/Scheme Manager**).

14 In the **Scheme Manager** dialog, click the **Edit** tab. In the **Background** section, select the **Use picture** checkbox and then click **Browse**.

15 In the **Import Picture** dialog:

- Browse to locate the image file you want to use for your background. (We chose a simple textile-effect image, but you can use any image you prefer.)

- Select the file, and then click **Open** to add the image as the background for your master page.

16 Back in the **Scheme Manager** dialog, click **OK**.

Your master page should now appear as illustrated.

Congratulations, your master page layout is complete. The advantage of using a master page for elements like this is that they will now appear on every page of our site—and we only had to set them up once!

Let's now move on to create the content on our other Web site pages. We'll begin by setting up our photo gallery on the **Collection** page.

We also added a copyright notice to our master page.

Setting up a photo gallery

We are now going to add a photo gallery using the Popup Rollover functionality in WebPlus.

1   On the **Site** tab, double-click the **Collection** page to open it in the workspace. Notice that your master page elements display on the page, but cannot be selected—they are safely stored away on the master page.

2   On the Web Objects toolbar, expand the Navigation flyout and click the 🔧 **Popup Rollover** button.

3   In the **Rollover Graphic** dialog **Browse** to select a 'Normal' image. Navigate to a folder containing the image that you want to add, and then select the image to open.

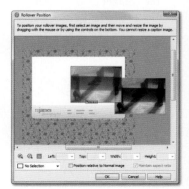

The 'Over' image will default to using the same file which is what we want.

4   Check the option to **Display caption with Over image**.

5   Type in a suitable caption to display when the image appears on the page. At this point, you can also change the text font, size and colour. However, for now leave it at the default.

6   Click **Set Rollover Position**.

A preview of the page will appear with the images randomly placed. You can zoom into the page by clicking 🔍.

7   Click on the image with the green border. This is the 'normal' image and will become our thumbnail. Change the **Left** alignment to 620 and the **Top** to about 66 pixels.

To change the size, simply change the **Width** to 50 pixels. The Height will change automatically providing **Maintain aspect ratio** is checked.

8   Next, click on the image with the blue outline, the Rollover image. We want this to appear towards the middle of the page and to be much larger than the thumbnail. Set the **Left** position to 325, **Top** to 120 and the **Width** to 250.

9   Click on the 'Caption' object with the red border. Drag it so that it is roughly in the centre of the image. Change the **Top** value to 350.

The dialog should now resemble the one on the right.

Click **OK** twice to close the dialogs.

10 Preview your page in your browser. Note that when you hover the mouse pointer over the thumbnail image, it displays the full size version with a caption.

Now all we need are some more images!

11 Close the preview to go back to your page. Repeat the process from step 2. You'll notice that the new images use the same **Left** and **Top** settings that you specified for your first rollover. This means that you may find that you only have to change the Width of the new images.

When you get back to your page for this time, you will see that the second thumbnail has been placed directly over the first. Click on the top image to select it and drag it down so that it is underneath the first thumbnail. At this stage, don't worry about the exact alignment as we will adjust this at the end.

Add five more images to your page by repeating steps 2-11.

> Avoid inserting large image files unnecessarily—for example, this might happen if your images are acquired directly from digital cameras set for high-resolution (2400 × 1800).
>
> With Serif PhotoPlus, you can reduce all image sizes in bulk (using a macro) before inserting them. Alternatively, use another photo editor to manually resize your images before creating your photo gallery.

12 Select your last thumbnail and drag it down so that it is just above the grey border of your navbar.

13 Now select all of your thumbnails.

14 On the **Align** tab, click 🔲 **Centre Horizontally** and 🔲 **Space Evenly Down**. The thumbnails should now be perfectly aligned.

15 Preview your results in a browser.

All we need now is some form of instruction to tell the visitor what to do. For this we need an HTML frame.

16 Click on the 🔳 **HTML Frame** tool and drag on the page to insert a frame that is approximately 220 × 50 pixels. Type:

Hover over a thumbnail to see a larger version of the image.

We used 12pt Arial for the font and set the text colour to light grey.

17 Select the HTML frame so that it is surrounded by a grey bounding box.

Use the **Transform** tab to set X to 330 pix and Y to 200 pix.

18 Finally, preview the page in your browser to see the effect.

Now when you hover over a thumbnail, the text will be hidden by the large image.

Great! We now have two of our Web pages in place. Let's move on to the **Equipment** page where we'll import some images and add hyperlinks to various equipment-related Web sites.

Importing images and creating hyperlinks

1 Open the **Equipment** page in the workspace by double-clicking it on the **Site** tab or selecting it from the Page Manager.

2 Use the **Quick Rectangle** tool to draw a rectangle on the page, approximately 200 pixels wide by 118 pixels high.

- Drag the left node down to round the corners.

- On the **Swatches** tab, apply a white fill and a light grey outline.

3 With the shape selected, click **Edit** and then click **Replicate...**.

> For tips on importing images and choosing export options, see the online Help or the "Importing Images" and "Creating Web-Friendly Sites" tutorials.

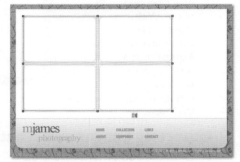

4   In the **Replicate** dialog:

  • Select **Create grid**.

  • Choose a 2 x 2 grid.

  • Select horizontal and vertical spacing of 10 pixels.

  • Click **OK**.

5   Move your grid into position on the **Equipment** page, as illustrated.

6   On the Standard Objects toolbar, click the 🖾 **Import Picture** button.

7   In the **Import Picture** dialog:

  • Browse to locate the image you want to import and select it.

  • Choose whether to embed or link the picture.

  • Click **Open**.

8   Click and drag on your page to insert the image inside the first square of your grid.

9   Repeat steps 6 to 8 to place images inside the other cells of your grid.

💡 **Optional step:** To create visual impact and variety, you can crop your images inside their grid cells.

To do this, select the image and then click the ☐ Crop tool. Click and drag the nodes to crop the image as desired.

Without crop

With crop

10 On the Standard Objects toolbar, click the 🔲 **HTML Frame** tool and draw a text frame—approximately 135 pixels wide by 35 pixels high—on your page.

11 Select the text object, then right-click and click **Copy**. Right-click again and click **Paste**. Repeat the **Copy** and **Paste** procedure to create a total of five identical text frames.

12 Drag the objects roughly into position one under the other, then click and drag a selection bounding box around them all.

13 On the **Align** tab:

* Click the **Left** align button.

* Select the **Spaced** check box and enter a value of 10 pixels.

* Click the **Space Evenly Down** button.

Your text frames are now precisely aligned and spaced.

14 Drag the group of text frames into place to the right of your image grid.

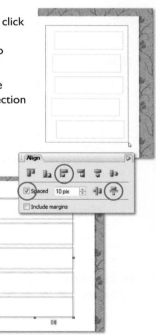

We used our text frames to display the names of various items of photography equipment and hyperlinks to relevant external Web sites.

15 Click inside a text frame and type a line of text followed by a Web site address of your choice.

Use the Text context toolbar and the **Swatches** (or **Colour**) tab to apply style and formatting of your choice.

16 To add a hyperlink, select the Web address and then on the Tools toolbar, on the Hyperlink flyout, click **Hyperlink** .

17 In the **Hyperlinks** dialog:

- Select the **Internet page** option.

- In the **Hyperlink Information** box, type the URL (Internet address) you want to link to.

- In the **Target Window or Frame** list, select **New Window**.

- Click **OK**.

18 Repeat steps 14 to 16 to add text and hyperlinks to the other text frames.

19 Preview the page in your browser and test your new hyperlinks!

We'll now create the **Contact** page. Here, we'll insert a simple Web-based form allowing visitors to the site to send their comments or questions to the photographer.

Creating a Form

1 Open the **Contact** page in the workspace by double-clicking it on the **Site** tab or selecting it from the Page Manager.

2 On the Web Objects toolbar, on the Forms flyout, click **Form Wizard**.

3 In the first Form Wizard dialog, click **Use and adapt a standard form** and then click **Next**.

4 The next dialog displays a list of predesigned form layouts. Click any list item to display a preview of the selected form in the **Preview** pane.

Select the **Comments 2** form and click **Next**.

The next dialog allows you to customize the form layout. Here, you can edit and delete the existing form controls, or add new ones.

5 The default form suits our purpose so click **Next** to proceed.

6 In the **Form Properties** dialog, on the **Action** tab:

- Select **An e-mail address**.

- Type a name for your form.

- Type the email address to which you want the site visitor's form data to be sent.

- Click **OK**.

7 To insert the form at default size, position the ⊕▦ cursor where you want the form to appear and then click the mouse button.

💡 The building blocks of a form comprise a mixture of text, graphics, and **form controls**.

Form controls collect Web visitor data and can be added, moved, and modified in a similar way to other WebPlus objects.

Form control fields include buttons, text boxes, check boxes, radio buttons, combo boxes, and so on. A typical form is made up of a combination of these fields.

Randomly generated graphic

Text input field

The Form options also include a CAPTCHA object. This is an anti-spamming control that can help to prevent junk email from non-human Web traffic. The site visitor must type the graphical word into the input field. If they match, the visitor is allowed to continue.

For detailed information, see "Adding forms" in online Help.

We're now going to adjust some of the elements on our form, so you might want to zoom in at this point.

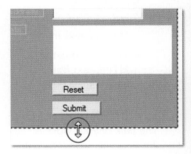

There are a couple of things we want to change:

Firstly, we're not happy with the position of the **Reset** and **Submit** buttons.

Secondly, we want to right-align the form field labels and change them all to lower-case letters.

WebPlus lets you move and edit form controls just as you would any other object. We'll demonstrate this now...

To move form buttons

- Click on each of the buttons in turn and drag them into place under the **Comments** text box, as illustrated.

  You may need to increase the size of the form to accommodate the new button placement—to do this, simply select the form and then click and drag a sizing handle.

  Select the buttons and the field text boxes and on the **Align** tab click the ☞ **Left** align button.

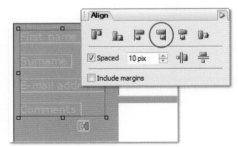

To align form field labels

- Select them all and then on the **Align** tab click the **Right** align button.

To edit and right-align field label text

- Double-click inside a text box and edit as you would any WebPlus text frame.

- With the text frame selected, on the Text context toolbar click the Align Right button.

8 Preview your form in your Web browser.

When site visitors view the site, they can type their details directly into the text boxes provided. When they click **Submit**, the information is sent to the email address you specify when creating the form.

9 To complete our **Contact** page:

- We created a title (Artistic text frame).

- We also added an HTML text frame containing a note written by the photographer.

The bulk of your work is done—congratulations! The remaining pages—**Home**, **About**, and **Links** can all be assembled using the techniques we've already discussed.

For information on the various types of text frames available in WebPlus, and when to use them, see the online Help or the "Getting Started: Working With Text" tutorial.

To conclude this project, we'll just summarize the procedures we used. If you need to refresh your memory, feel free to return to the step-by-step instructions provided earlier in the exercise.

The Home page

On our **Home** page, we wanted the focus to be on the 'photo of the week.'

- We used the basic  **Import Picture** tool to place our image.

- We used an HTML text frame to display information about the image.

The About page

On our **About** page, a large HTML text frame contains a message from the photographer.

What inspires me as a photographer? That's not an easy question to answer but fundamental to what drives my passion for photography.

I am inspired by the beauty of the natural world and at the same time by the more industrial, impersonal nature of the manmade world, even to the extent of recording the most mundane aspects of daily life. On a more sentimental level it could be recording special moments in my life with family and friends.

Film or digital photography? They both have their advantages. It all depends on what you photograph and what message you want to relate. Film, particularly black and white film, can capture—even create—a particular mood which is difficult to replicate in the digital medium. Digital photography is convenient and allows inexpensive experimentation.

I ultimately pursue photography for my own interest, however, I am very pleased if others derive pleasure from it.

The Links page

Our **Links** page contains a series of HTML text frames displaying hyperlinks to other useful photography-related sites.

That's it! You've finally reached the end of this exercise. We think you'll agree that it was not too difficult a task.

We hope that you have enjoyed creating this simple yet effective Web site, and are feeling confident enough to create your own personal site from scratch. If you would like to develop your site further by adding dynamic objects, such as hit counters, blogs, and shout boxes, move on to the "Creating Personal Web Sites: Adding Dynamic Content to Your Site" tutorial.

Adding Dynamic Content to Your Site

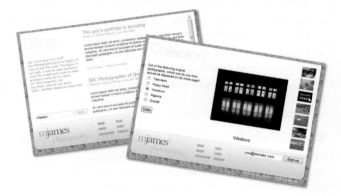

This project assumes that you have completed the "Creating a Personal Web Site" tutorial and are now ready to add dynamic and interactive content to your site.

If you haven't worked through the "Creating a Personal Web Site" tutorial you can apply the procedures described here to any of your existing Web sites, or create a new one.

In this project, you'll learn how to:

- Sign up for Serif Web Resources.
- Insert and configure WebPlus Smart objects—a hit counter, blog, shout box, poll, and subscription box.
- Edit and manage Smart objects.

160 | **Tutorials**
Adding Dynamic Content to Your Site

Adding Dynamic Content to Your Site

Our photographer client has decided to develop his Web site further and add some interactive and dynamic features. He has given us the following list of requirements:

- He wants to know how many visitors his site is attracting so has asked for a **hit counter**.
- He wants to allow visitors to sign up to a **mailing list**.
- He wants viewers to vote for the photograph they think should be displayed on the **Home** page. We'll use a **poll** for this.
- He wants to create 'articles' on the site and allow viewers to add their own comments—this calls for a **blog**.
- Finally, he'd like his site visitors to be able to chat to each other, and to him, in 'real-time' using a **shout box**.

This sounds like a long and complicated wish list, but you'll be pleased to know that all of these features are supported by WebPlus X2. What's more they are easy to create!

Serif Web Resources and Smart Objects

WebPlus provides a range of interactive and dynamic objects, such as those listed above, which all 'collect' information from the object. These objects are known as **Smart objects** and are available from **Serif Web Resources**, a secure online service which not only 'hosts' the objects, but also stores the associated data on secure server space designated to Serif.

Setting up a Serif Web Resources account

To access the Smart objects, you need to log in to Serif Web Resources. If you don't have a valid username and password you must first create a Serif Web Resources account.

1: To create a Serif Web Resources account

1 On the Web Objects toolbar, click the 🌐 **Smart Object** tool.

2 In the login dialog, click **Create Account**.

3   In the next dialog:

   • Type your email address.

   • Type your password twice.

   • Click **Signup**.

   An additional dialog asks you for additional personal details.

   You can also select check boxes if you want to receive the Serif Community newsletter, Serif offers, and/or third-party offers.

4   A confirmation email is sent to your email address.

   Click the link in the email and you're ready to access Web Resources!

> **Create a Serif Web Resources Account**
>
> To create an account with Serif Web Resources, you will need the following:
>
> a.) A working email address.
> b.) If the email address specified in a.) is not associated with a Serif account, you will need to provide extra information in order to create your Web Resources account.
>
> Please complete the form below, then press the Signup button. A confirmation email will be sent to the address specified - you must click the link in the email to activate your new account. If you do not respond to the email within 24 hours, you will need to complete the form again.
>
> ☐ Check this box if you agree to the Terms And Conditions.
>
> Email Address
> seriftest@serif.com
>
> Choose a password   Retype the password
> ••••••••••   ••••••••••
>
> [Signup] [Cancel]

> **ℹ Creating a Serif Web Resources account**
>
> If your email address is known to Serif (you've previously registered), you'll be asked a few questions to complete registration.
>
> If your email address is unknown to Serif (you're new to Serif or unregistered), you must complete full security. Follow the instructions on the login screens.

2: To access Serif Web Resources

1   On the Web Objects toolbar, click the the 🐾 **Smart Object** tool.

2   In the login dialog:

   • Type your username (email address).

   • Type your password.

   • **Optional:** To access Serif Web Resources directly in future, bypassing the login screen, select **Remember account details**.

   • Click the **Login** button.

The **Smart Objects** dialog opens.

Note that Smart objects are not added directly to the page from Serif Web Resources, but are first added to an object library displayed in the left **My Smart Objects** pane. Currently, because we have yet to create any Smart objects, the library is empty.

The Smart objects library lets you manage and edit your objects and add them to your Web pages immediately or later.

We're now ready to create our Smart objects.

Creating and inserting Smart objects

In this section, we'll add five Smart objects to our site. We'll begin by adding a simple hit counter.

We added our hit counter to the **Home** page of our site—so if you're following our example, open this page in the workspace. Alternatively, you can work through this example using any Web page.

To add a hit counter to the library

1 In the **Smart Objects** dialog, beneath the **My Smart Objects** pane, click **New**.

2 In the **Create Smart Object** dialog, select the **Hit Counter** option and click **OK**.

3 In the **Create New Hit Counter** dialog:

   • Select a hit counter style.

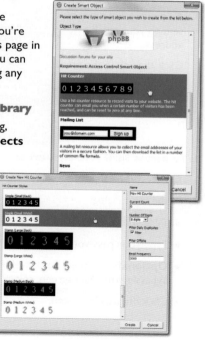

- Type a name for your hit counter.

- Choose the number of digits to display.

- To ensure that multiple visits made by the same visitor in one day are only counted as a single hit, select **Filter Daily Duplicates**.

- In the **Email Frequency** box, specify how often you want to be notified of the count. For example, type '1000,' to receive email notification each time the counter increments by a multiple of 1000.

- Click **Create to** add the hit counter object to the library.

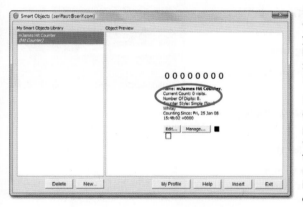

In the **My Smart Objects** dialog, your hit counter is listed in the **My Smart Objects Library** pane.

Notice that the **Object Preview** pane displays the **Current count** for the site. This number will increment with the counter.

To add a hit counter to the page

1 In the **Smart Objects Library**, select the hit counter and click **Insert**.

Position the ⁺▦ cursor where you want the hit counter to appear and then click on the page. The hit counter previews automatically.

0 0 0 0 0 0 0 0

> 💡 If your Smart objects do not preview on the page, you can turn previews on.
>
> **To turn Smart object previews on:**
>
> 1 Click **Tools**, then **Options**.
>
> 2 In the **Options** dialog, select **UI Settings** and then select the **Smart Object Previews** check box.

Great, we've added our first Smart object. We can use the same procedure to add the other Smart objects to our site.

Next, we'll add a mailing list to the master page—this will allow visitors to sign up from any page on the site.

To add a mailing list

1   Open the master page and click the 🔅 **Smart Object** tool.

2   In the **Smart Objects** dialog, click **New**.

3   In the **Create Smart Object** dialog:

  • Select **Mailing List**.

  • Choose a **Language** option.

  • Click **OK**.

4   In the **Create New Mailing List** dialog:

  • Type a name for the mailing list.

  • Click **Create** to add the mailing list object to your library.

5   Click **Insert** and add the mailing list to your page.

6   **Optional step:** Add a text frame inviting your viewers to sign up to the mailing list.

The next item on our 'to do' list is a poll. In our example, we placed this on our photo gallery page.

To add a poll

1   Click the 🔅 **Smart Objects** tool.

2   In the **Smart Objects** dialog, click **New**.

3   In the **Create Smart Object** dialog, select **Poll**, choose a **Language** option, and then click **OK**.

4 In the **Create New Poll** dialog:

- In the text box at the top of the dialog, type your poll question.

- In the boxes below, type the voting options you want to display.

- Use the other controls to adjust the appearance of the poll. You can change text colour, font, and size.

- Click **Create** to add the poll object to your library.

5 Click **Insert** to add the poll to your page.

6 Preview the page in your browser to see how your poll will appear to site visitors.

We'll show you how to view the results of your poll later, but first we still have some Smart objects to create...

We've decided to replace the **Equipment** page of our Web site with a **Blog** page. Here, we'll insert both a blog and a shout box.

To update page details

1   Instead of deleting the **unwanted** page and creating a new one from scratch, you can simply delete the contents from the page and then reset the page properties in the **Page Properties** dialog.

    (To open the **Page Properties** dialog, right-click the page on the **Site** tab and click **Page Properties**.)

2   Next, on the navbar, select the 'old' Equipment button and click the ⬚T Theme Graphic Edit button.

3   In the **Theme Graphic Settings** dialog, type the new name for the button.

    No need to edit the hyperlink between the button and the page as WebPlus automatically does this for us.

    We're ready to create our final Smart objects...

To add a blog

1   Click the 🌸 **Smart Objects** tool and in the **Smart Objects** dialog, click **New**.

2   In the **Create Smart Object** dialog, select **Blog**, select a **Language** option, and click **OK**.

3 In the **Create New Blog** dialog:

- Type a name and description for the blog.

- Use the controls at the right of the dialog, to adjust the appearance of the blog (body and info text colour, font style and size, and border colour and thickness).

The **Blog Preview** pane updates as you make your changes.

4 Select your time zone from the drop-down list.

5 **Optional:** Under the **Name** and **Description** boxes, the following settings are provided:

- **Blogger Name**, **Description**, and **Photograph URL**: Use these boxes to provide additional 'profile' information about the blog and its author.

- **Alternative style sheet (CSS) URL**: To change the layout and presentation of your blog using a custom style sheet, type the URL of the style sheet .css file into this box.

- **Layout**: To hide the header and/or sidebar of the blog, select the relevant check box(es).

6 **Optional:** In the **Blog Settings** section, the following check boxes are provided:

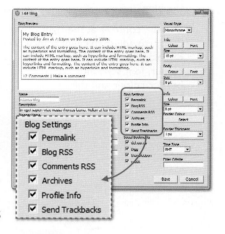

- **Permalink**: Select to add a hyperlink beneath each blog article, allowing blog users to 'bookmark' an article and return to it later.

- **Blog RSS**: Select to include an RSS feed for the blog, allowing blog readers to keep up-to-date with the most recent blog articles.

- **Comments RSS**: Select to include an RSS feed for each blog article. This is a particularly useful for blogs containing very popular and 'active' articles, where blog users want to be informed of new comments that have been added to an article.

- **Archives**: Select to provide blog readers with access to monthly archives of blog articles.

- **Profile Info**: Select/clear this option to display/hide the blogger profile information specified in step 4.

- **Send Trackbacks**: Select to scan new blog articles for links to other blogs, then automatically notify the blog that it has been referenced (using standard 'trackback' and 'pingback' protocols).

- The **Social Bookmarks** section lets you provide blog users with the ability to submit articles to popular social bookmarking sites.

7 When you are
happy with your
blog settings, click
Create to add the
blog object to
your **Smart
Objects Library**.

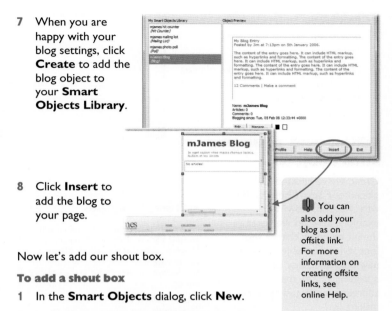

8 Click **Insert** to
add the blog to
your page.

Now let's add our shout box.

To add a shout box

1 In the **Smart Objects** dialog, click **New**.

2 In the **Create Smart Object** dialog, select
Shout Box and click **OK**.

3 In the **Create New Shout
Box** dialog:

  • Type a name for the shout
    box.

  • Use the controls to set the
    appearance of the
    shout box.

  • Click **Create** to add
    the shout box object to
    your library.

  • Click **Insert** and add
    the shout box to your
    page.

> You can
> also add your
> blog as on
> offsite link.
> For more
> information on
> creating offsite
> links, see
> online Help.

4 Preview the Smart objects on your new **Blog** page in your Web browser.

(Your page will not look like ours as you do not yet have any blog or shout box entries yet.)

Editing and managing Smart objects

Great, we've created and placed our Smart objects. But what happens now? For example, how do we reset the hit counter, change the font style of an object, add a new blog article or poll question, or see the addresses collected by our mailing list?

We'll now show you how to edit and manage Smart objects. We'll focus on our hit counter, blog, and mailing list objects, but the same principles apply for all objects.

> **Editing Smart objects**
>
> Most of the dialog options for editing and creating a Smart object are the same. However, note that the object's **Name** is not editable—this option is 'read only' and displayed as 'greyed out' in the edit dialogs.
>
> **To edit an object on the page:**
> - Double-click the object, or right-click and select **Edit Smart Object**.
>
> **To edit an object in the library:**
> - Select it and then in the **Object Preview** pane, click **Edit**.

You can edit Smart objects in the Smart Object Library or directly on the page.

To edit a hit counter

1 In the WebPlus workspace, right-click the hit counter and select **Edit Smart Object**.

2 In the **Edit Hit Counter** dialog you can:

- Change the appearance of the counter.

- Reset the count to zero and the 'Counting Since' time to the current time.

> Counting Since
> **Tue, 05 Feb 08 14:48:03 +0000**
>
> To reset the count to zero, and set the "Counting Since" time to now, press the button below.
>
> Reset

Due to the nature of blogs, you'll probably want to manage these objects quite frequently. For example, to add new articles or even delete comments posted by site visitors (hopefully you won't need to do this too often!).

To manage a blog

1   Click the 🐝 **Smart Objects** tool.

2   In the **Smart Objects Library**, select the blog then in the **Object Preview** pane click **Manage**.

3   In the **Manage Blog** dialog, several options are available.

To create a new blog article:

- Click **New**.

- Type your article title in the **Article Title** box.

- Type your article content in the main window. To format the text, use the toolbar controls.

- To categorize your article and allow blog users to search for similar articles of interest, type tag keywords into the **Tags** box. (For a list of suggested tags, click the **suggest** link.)

- If you want your blog to receive trackbacks, posting references from other blog sites as a comment on the referenced article, select the **Allow Trackbacks** check box.

💡 New to WebPlus X2 is the ability to control who is permitted to post comments to your blog articles. For example, you can:

- Prevent spam by using a CAPTCHA control.

- Restrict access by granting access to specific user groups

For details, see "Access control" in online Help.

• Click **Save** to add the new article and return to the **Manage Blog** dialog.

(You'll see your new article listed.)

To edit an existing article:

• Select the article and click **Edit**. Make your changes and click **Save**.

To delete an existing article:

• Select the article and click **Delete**.

To edit article comments:

• Select the article and click **Comments**. You can delete selected comments for an article, or clear all comments.

💡 You can also remove unwanted lines of text from your shout boxes.

To remove a shout box entry:

• In the **Manage Shout Box** dialog, click the word '**Delete**' next to the unwanted entry.

Mailing lists can be used for many purposes. For example, you can ask your site visitors to sign up for newsletters, special event notifications, information requests, and so on. Of course, you'll need to access this list of addresses in order to make use of it! Again, WebPlus makes it easy to manage the data collected in your mailing list objects.

To manage a mailing list

1 Repeat steps 1 and 2 of the previous procedure to open the **Manage Mailing List** dialog.

The **Manage Mailing List** dialog displays a list of all the email addresses collected. :

- To delete an individual address, click **Delete**.

- To remove all entries from the list, click **Clear All**.

- To add all of the email addresses from your mailing list to your Access Control accounts, click **Sync to Accounts**, then select the Access Control account from the drop-down list.

(This will automatically give everyone on the list a username they can use to log into your site.)

As previously mentioned, the editing/managing process is the same for all Smart objects. Why not try this now by adding a new poll option, or creating some shout box text entries and then deleting them.

Well, that concludes this project. If you want to take things further—
allowing visitors to make online purchases from your Web site—see the
"Creating Business Web Sites: Creating an E-Commerce Web Site"
tutorial.

Adding Flash™ Objects to Your Site

The WebPlus **Gallery** tab provides a wide range of predesigned Flash™ banners that you can add to your site, and customize to suit your needs.

In addition, it's very easy to add your own custom Flash objects to your WebPlus site.

In this tutorial we'll show you how to:

- Insert a custom Flash object into a WebPlus document.
- Fine-tune your Flash object.
- Add a predesigned WebPlus Flash banner to your site.

Flash Objects

Flash™ (*.swf) files are viewable movies using the Flash™ Player format. In WebPlus X2, you can see the effects of these files as soon as they are placed on your page, even without previewing.

To insert a custom Flash™ file

1   Open an existing WebPlus site, or create a new blank site.

2   On the **Insert** menu, choose **Media**, and then click **Flash**.

- or -

On the Web Objects toolbar, on the **Media** flyout, click ⬤ **Insert Flash File**.

3   In the **Flash** dialog, click **Browse**, and then locate and select the .swf file you want to insert.

You will find an example, **DaftDog.swf**, in your **Workspace** folder. In a standard installation, you'll find this in the following location:

C:\Program Files\Serif\WebPlus\X2\Tutorials\Workspace

To keep the .swf file separate from the WebPlus file (using a link to the source file) clear the **Embed Flash file in site** option.

Optional step: You can also fine-tune your Flash™ object in this dialog.

For example, you can choose to:

• Start the animation as soon as the page is loaded.

• Loop the animation.

• Set background transparency.

• Add parameters—advanced functionality allowing modification of the object's behaviour on the completed page.

4   When you have selected the required options, click **OK**.

5   On the WebPlus page, you'll see the
    Picture Import cursor.

    Click to insert the file at its default size, or drag
    to set a custom size. You should see a preview
    of the file as you drag.

    Remember, you can always resize a Flash
    object once you have placed it on your page.

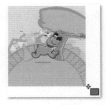

Note that the valid
parameters for Flash™ objects
vary depending on the object
itself. For details, see the
documentation relating to your
particular Flash object.

Congratulations! You have successfully
added the Flash object to your Web
site. Feel free to preview it in your
favourite browser.
Should you choose to publish your site
to the Internet, WebPlus will
automatically upload your Flash object
for you; no additional work is required
on your behalf.

Flash Banners

Web banners can be useful advertising tools. The following section
shows you how to add and customize a predesigned WebPlus Flash
banner on your site's master page.

To insert a predesigned Flash banner

1   Open the master page of your site and click
    the **Gallery** tab.

2   At the top of the tab, expand the **WebPlus
    Gallery** folder, and then expand **Template
    Flash Banners**.

3   Expand the **1 Image** category and then click
    on the **Slide in with flicker** subcategory.
    The lower section of the tab now displays
    thumbnails of the various banner styles
    available.

4   Click on the **Photographer** thumbnail and
    drag it onto your master page.

5   Select the banner then on the **Align** tab, click  **Centre Horizontally**.

Currently, the title of the banner displays the company title that is set in the WebPlus **User Details** dialog.

Unless you have already edited the user details, the title displayed by default will be '**Your Company Name**'.

You can change this text by either updating the user details, or by editing the Flash banner. We'll show both methods.

To update the banner title by setting user details

1   Click outside of the page area to deselect everything, then on the Page context toolbar, click
     🔍🔍 Set User Details.

2   In the **User Details** dialog, change the company name to any name of your choice and click **Update**.

The banner updates with your new company name.

💡 Store frequently-used or frequently-updated information in the **User Details** dialog. It will make updating data like mobile phone numbers or email addresses much easier! To insert a **user details** item:

1   Create a text frame on your page.

2   On the **Insert** menu, choose **Information**, then click **User Details**.

3   In the **User Details** dialog, select the line of text you want to insert and then click **OK**.

The **User Details** dialog is great for updating some text elements on your banner, such as your company name, address, or telephone number. But suppose you want to change the image—for example, to display a new product—or edit the bullet points to reflect recent new features or special offers.

To edit Flash banner elements

1   Double-click the banner, or right-click and select **Edit Flash**.

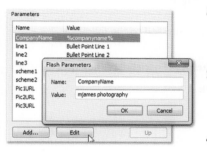

2   In the **Flash** dialog, in the **Parameters** pane, click to select the **CompanyName** element and then click the **Edit** button.

3   In the **Flash Parameters** dialog, in the **Value** box, delete the text (including the %) and type your company name. Click **OK**.

4   Repeat steps 2 and 3 to edit the bullet point text (line1, line2, and line3) as required.

5   When you've finished updating your text elements, click **OK** to close the **Flash** dialog and review your changes.

There may be times when you want to change other elements of your banner, such as the image, or even the colours.

You can use the same dialog to do this, as we'll now demonstrate.

6   Double-click the banner to open the **Flash** dialog.

7   In the right of the dialog, the **Additional Files** box lists the images used in the banner. (This particular banner only uses one image; others may use more.)

Click the **Add** button and then brows to the mjames sample photo images provided in your ...**Workspace\mjames** folder.

💡 As this banner only uses one image, the image at the top of the list is the one that is displayed. We suggest you delete any unused files from the **Additional Files** list. While any 'extra' images will not display, they will still be included when you publish your site and will therefore take up Web server space unnecessarily.

For banners using two or three images, the images are displayed in the order they are listed in the **Additional Files** box.

In a standard installation, this folder is installed to the following location:

C:\Program Files\Serif\WebPlus\X2\Tutorials\Workspace

8   Select the **clouds.png** file and click **Open**.

The new file is added to the **Additional Files** list.

9   Select the **clouds.png** file in the list and click the **Up** button to move it to the top of the list.

10 Click **OK** to see your new image displayed in the banner.

Two and three image banners

The steps for inserting two and three image banners are very similar to adding a one image banner, there are just a couple of additional images!

1   Open a new site by choosing **File > New**.

2   From the **Gallery** tab, expand **Template Flash Banners > 2 Image** category and click on the **Slide in with Flicker Image Swap** subcategory.

3 Click on the **Photographer** thumbnail and drag it onto your master page.

You will notice that the banner has retained the User settings that you edited in the previous section.

4 Double-click the banner to open the **Flash Parameters** dialog.

5 In the **Additional Files** section on the right you'll see two .jpg files listed.

These are the image files that are currently displayed in the banner.

Click the **Add** button and then in the **Open** dialog, browse to your **Tutorials\Workspace** folder. In a standard installation, this folder is installed to the following location:

C:\Program Files\Serif\WebPlus\X2\Tutorials\Workspace

Select the **poppy head.png** file and click **Open**.

6 The new file is now listed in the **Additional Files** list box. Select it and click **Up** twice to move it to the top of the list.

7 Repeat steps **6-7** to add **droplet.png**.

8 To get the Flash banner to loop, ensure that the **Loop** option is checked.

9 Click **OK** and review your changes on the page.

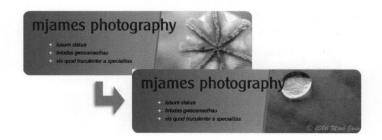

Editing the banner colour scheme

1   Double-click the banner to reopen the **Flash** dialog.

2   In the parameters list, you'll see two elements labelled **scheme1** and **scheme2**. These elements link to colour swatches in the site's currently selected colour scheme.

We'll return to WebPlus colour schemes in more detail later. For the following steps, all you need to know is that the currently selected scheme colours for this site are displayed as numbered swatches at the bottom of the **Swatches** tab.

Parameters	
Name	Value
CompanyName	mjames photography
line1	lusum statua
line2	briodas gwasanaethau
line3	vis quod truculenter a spe...
scheme1	%scheme5%
scheme2	%scheme3%
Pic1URL	%file1%
Pic2URL	%file2%
Pic3URL	%file3%

3   In the **Parameters** pane, select the **scheme1** element and click **Edit**.

4   In the **Flash Parameters** dialog, change the value to **%scheme5%**. Click **OK**.

5   Repeat the steps to change **scheme 2** to **%scheme3%**.

6   Click **OK** to close the **Flash** dialog and view your results.

You'll see that the text elements have been updated with your changes. In addition, the company name is now sitting on a green background, which corresponds to the **Scheme Colour 4** swatch on the **Swatches** tab.

By choosing scheme colours in this way, the Flash banner will also update whenever you change the colour scheme of the site.

These are just some of the things you can do with the banners. Feel free to experiment on your own, or for another hands-on example, see "Getting Started: Theme Graphics and the Gallery".

Adding a Flash™ Photo Gallery

With WebPlus X2, you can now add Flash™ photo galleries to your Web sites. Simply add your photos, and then choose from a range of professionally-designed templates. You can customize the templates to suit the theme of your photos, and even add background music!

In this tutorial, we'll show you how to:

- Add images to a photo gallery.
- Add photo captions.
- Apply gallery styles and settings.
- Edit an existing photo gallery.
- Password protect the page containing your photo gallery.

Adding a Flash Photo Gallery

In this exercise, we'll create a photo gallery using photographs taken on a visit to the zoo. If you want to use the same images, you'll find them in your **Workspace\Zoo** folder. In a standard installation, this folder is installed to the following location:

C:\Program Files\Serif\WebPlus\X2\Workspace\Zoo

We'll create our gallery on a new blank Web site, but you may want to add yours to an existing WebPlus project.

1   From the Startup Wizard, click **Create New > Blank Site**, or on the Standard toolbar, click ☐ **New Site**.

2   On the Standard Objects toolbar, on the 🖾 ▾ Picture flyout, click
    🖾 **Flash Photo Gallery**.

3   In the **Flash Photo Gallery** dialog, click **Add Folder**.

4   In the **Browse for Folder** dialog, select the folder containing your images and click **OK**.

💧 The **Flash Photo Gallery** dialog offers the following options for adding images:

• **Add Files:** Choose this option to add individual images to your gallery.

• **Add Folder:** Choose this option to add images contained inside a folder on your computer.

• **Add Twain:** Choose this option to add images from a TWAIN source, such as a scanner or digital camera. (For details, see online Help.)

Your images
display as
thumbnails in
the dialog.

5 You can use
the buttons
running down
the left side of
the dialog to
add more
images or
delete images
that you no
longer want.

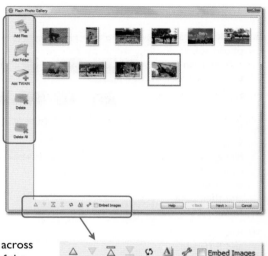

6 Use the buttons across
the lower edge of the
dialog to adjust image
order, rotate images, add captions, make image adjustments, and
embed images.

We want our photo gallery to begin with the photo of the giraffe's
head. Currently this photo is last in the sequence so we need to
move it.

7 Select the
photo and
then click △
**Move to
Front**.

Now let's add some captions to our photos.

8 With the first
photo still
selected, on
the lower
toolbar, click
△ **Caption**.

9 In the
Caption
dialog, type a
caption for the
selected photo
and then click
OK.

10 Repeat steps 8
and 9 to add
captions to the remaining photos.

11 **Optional:** To embed your images in the .wpp project file, select the
Embed Images check box. (If you do not select this option your
images will remain 'linked' to the file.)

12 When you are happy with your images and captions, click **Next**.

13 Click through
the templates
displayed in the
Gallery Style
pane.

As you do so:

• The **Preview**
pane shows
how your
photos will
appear with
the selected
gallery style
applied.

- The **Settings** pane updates to display the various options you can adjust for the selected gallery style.

14 Select the gallery style you prefer and then adjust the settings as required.

15 When you are happy with your photo gallery style and settings, click **Finish**.

- or -

To add or remove photos, click **Back** to return to the previous dialog. Make your changes, click **Next**, and then click **Finish**.

Settings
Background Music
None
Thumbnails
8
Font Colour

Blur Amount
20
☑ Thumbnail Rollovers
☑ Thumbnail Borders
☐ Large Control Bar
☐ Auto Hide Control Bar
☐ Auto Play
Duration
5

16 To insert the photo gallery at default size, simply click on the page.

- or -

To set the size of the photo gallery yourself, click and drag with the Picture Import cursor.

17 To preview your photo gallery:

On the Standard toolbar, click **HTML Preview** and select **Preview in Window**.

18 To switch between your working page and the preview window, click the tabs at the top of the workspace.

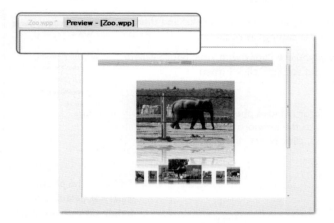

Once you've inserted your photo gallery, it's easy to add and delete photos, switch to a different gallery style, and adjust settings.

Let's take a look at this now.

To edit a Flash Photo Gallery

1 Right click the photo gallery and click **Edit Photo Gallery**.

2 The **Flash Photo Gallery** dialog opens.

3 Follow the steps outlined previously to fine-tune your gallery.

We've reached the end of this tutorial. In a few simple steps, we've created a stylish, professional-looking photo gallery. We're sure you'll enjoy experimenting with this powerful new feature—a great way to display treasured memories, or showcase those artistic shots you're particularly proud of!

Creating Business Web Sites

In the following tutorials, the focus is on creating and enhancing business sites. However, many of the techniques and features illustrated can be used just as effectively on a personal Web site.

- Setting Up a Commercial Web Site
- Creating an E-Commerce Web Site
- Adding a Forum
- Adding an Image Catalogue
- Optimizing Your Site for Search Engines

Setting Up a Commercial Web Site

Suppose you already have a Web site that you've created for a hobby or subject of interest. Now you want to take the next step and start up a small online business. In this tutorial, we'll provide information, guidelines, and useful tips to help you set up a commercial Web site.

Topics discussed include the following:

- Creating a Web identity
- Identifying your target market
- Defining goals and business needs
- Registering domain names
- Choosing a Web host provider
- Using multiple email accounts
- Optimizing for search engines

Setting Up a Commercial Web Site

Today, it's very rare to find a business that doesn't have some kind of Web presence. Whether your company is small or large, whether you intend to sell your products or services over the Web or just promote them, a Web site allows you to reach a much wider audience than is possible using more traditional methods.

Over recent years, setting up a Web site has become a much less complicated process. Since the first release of WebPlus, the Serif Development team has worked hard to make the program easy to use and accessible to even the novice user. In addition, Web hosting providers offer a wide range of low cost packages to help you get up and running.

However, creating an effective commercial Web presence requires more than just creating, registering, and hosting your site—it involves careful planning. In particular, you need to give some thought to your Web 'identity,' audience, goals, and business needs. We'll take at look at these areas first, and then move on to discuss domain names, Web host providers, and other commercial Web site considerations.

Creating a Web identity

Your **Web identity** refers to the way in which your business presents itself, and delivers its message, in printed and online media. The main elements of Web identity include:

- Your logo

- The mood, look, and feel of your site (for example, colour, font style, and layout)

- Any other elements that make up your corporate image (brochures, catalogues, flyers, and so on)

- The way in which you present text and graphical content (do you want to convey a formal, business-like approach or a more casual one?)

While there are no set rules for developing a Web identity, the most successful ones are **simple** and **recognizable**, **homogenous**—aim for a consistent message throughout your site, and have **staying power** (it is desirable to be modern and current, but not so much so that your Web identity may quickly go out of fashion).

The following WebPlus templates present very different Web identities.

Example 1

A clean and simple, no-frills layout with a clear message. We immediately know what this Web site is selling, and how we can buy it.

The 'more info' links keep the page content to a minimum, but make it easy for visitors to find additional information if required.

Example 2

A fun, modern, trendy, site that offers a wide range of products, services, links, and interactive content.

Web sites like this one can be confusing so it's important to have a structured layout. Here, the columnar layout and simple colour scheme give order and consistency to an otherwise busy site.

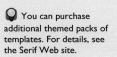 You can purchase additional themed packs of templates. For details, see the Serif Web site.

Getting the message across

Your Web site should help people understand what product or service you provide, and why they should buy it. Put yourself in the position of a first-time visitor to the site and ask yourself the following questions:

- Who is the company or person behind the site?
- What are they trying to promote or sell?
- Are they offering me something that their competitors aren't?
- Is the subject of each Web page clear?
- If applicable, is it easy to buy the product or service?
- Is it easy to navigate the pages of the site?
- Is it clear where I should go to find more information?

Using colour and special effects

The rule of thumb is 'keep it simple.'

Pick a simple colour scheme and use it consistently throughout your site. If you don't know where to start, take a look at other Web sites to get a feel for what works and what doesn't.

For a detailed discussion of colour schemes, see the "Getting Started: Working With Colour Schemes" tutorial.

WebPlus provides a range of predesigned colour schemes, which you can apply to your site.

To select a colour scheme:

1 Click the **Swatches** tab.

At the bottom of the tab, the five main colours in the current scheme appear as numbered samples, from 1 to 5, You'll also see additional samples labelled **H** (Hyperlink), **F** (Followed hyperlink), **A** (Active hyperlink), R (Rollover hyperlink), **B** (Background colour), and **O** (On-page colour), which apply to hyperlink, background, and page colours.

2 On the context toolbar, click the **Colour Scheme** button to open the **Scheme Manager**.

3 Select a different colour scheme from the list and click **OK**. Any regions in the site that have been assigned one of the colour scheme numbers are updated with the corresponding colour from the new scheme.

For more information, see online Help.

Avoid adding too many special effects as they can distract viewers from the content of the site. (Note also that files containing spinning or flashing effects tend to be very large and can take a while to download, which can be irritating for visitors.)

Identifying your target market

If you have an established business, you should already be very familiar with your customer base and target market.

If you're just starting out, you'll need to establish not only who your potential customers are, but why they should choose your product rather than your competitors' (for example, you may be offering a unique feature, a personalized service, or free delivery).

> The UK government's Business Link Web site at **http://www.businesslink.gov.uk** is a great resource—both for those who already have their online business up and running, and for those who are just starting out.
>
> You'll find a wealth of information and advice, including topics such as customer needs assessment; business plan preparation; sales and marketing strategies; tax considerations; IT and e-Commerce; as well as links to local trade associations, market research reports, and case studies.

The more you know about your customers and their needs, the more successfully you'll be able to market your product to them.

Similarly, you should have a thorough knowledge of your competitors and the products and services they are offering. You can use this information to help you market, develop, and improve your product, and ensure you continue to respond quickly to market needs and trends.

Defining goals and business needs

If you've put together a solid business plan, you should have realistic strategies and objectives for business development and growth. You'll also be aware of your business requirements.

Your business requirements may comprise staffing, premises, IT, and so on, but should also include Web site requirements such as Web space and transfer bandwidth requirements, security, e-Commerce shopping cart provider, payment options, email accounts, and so on.

With this information to hand, you'll be better equipped to design and implement your site, and also choose the most suitable Web host provider (we'll discuss this later).

Registering domain names

Simply put, your domain name serves as the unique identifier or 'address' of your Web site on the Internet.

For example, in Serif's Web site address
http://www.serif.com/store/index.asp
the domain name is **serif.com**.

It's very easy and inexpensive to register a domain name, and there are numerous **domain name registrars** that offer this service.

In most cases, a domain name registrar will charge a registry fee for one year. This means that you 'own' your domain name for one year, and must renew your subscription annually to maintain ownership. At the end of this period, you can choose to renew your registration with the same domain name registrar, transfer the domain name to a different registrar, or cancel the registration—if you choose the latter then your domain name becomes available for others to adopt.

> All domain name registrations are stored in a central domain name registry, which is also known as the Network Information Centre (NIC).
>
> When you register a domain name, the domain name registrar first checks the availability of the name by conducting a search of the NIC.

To prevent other businesses from registering the same domain name with a different extension, consider registering multiple domain name extensions—for example, mySite.com, mySite.net, and so on. Don't worry, you don't have to have a different Web site for each extension, you can simply have them all mapped to the same address (if you don't believe us, try typing "http://www.serif.co.uk" into your Web browser!). Most domain name registrars offer this service (called **DNS mapping**) for a small cost.

Choosing a Web host provider

Simply put, Web host providers allow you to lease space on their **Web server**(s)—complex computers that require specialist server software and technical expertise, and are connected to the Internet 24 hours a day, 7 days a week. The Web server stores all of the files necessary to display the pages of your Web site.

While it's relatively easy to find inexpensive Web hosting, each provider will offer a variety of different packages, and each package will differ in the quality of features and technical support offered. Choosing the best package for your site can be a daunting task; however, if you've determined your business needs, you'll have a good idea of the features you're looking for and the level of support you require.

One of the main decisions you need to make is whether you want **shared** (also called **virtual**), **dedicated**, or **managed** hosting.

- In **shared hosting**, you share the services of the Web host with other Web sites. If you're working with a limited budget, shared hosting is the best option.

  There are some risks and limitations to shared hosting (described below), however, and you need to decide whether or not these are important to you.

- In **dedicated hosting**, the Web server, related software, and Internet connection are reserved for your Web site only. In addition, you control the configuration and day-to-day management of the server and software. Dedicated hosting is generally preferred by companies who anticipate a high volume of Web traffic, and who require total control. For obvious reasons, this option is more expensive than shared hosting.

- **Managed hosting** offers a dedicated Web server and Internet connection along with some of the services included in the shared-host packages. Consider this solution if you need an exclusive Web server, but don't want to get involved in server/software configuration, administration, security, and so on. Managed Web host providers usually offer a

> If you already have an Internet Service Provider, you will probably have free space allocated for a personal Web site.
>
> If your Web site is a relatively small one, and you don't need a lot of transfer bandwidth, you can choose to direct your domain name to this free Web space. However, if you are concerned about space and bandwidth restrictions, then it's probably a good idea to pay for the services of a Web host provider.
>
> For information about accessing your free Web space, see the "Getting Started: Accessing Your Free Web Space" tutorial.

range of features, which you can mix and match to suit your needs. This type of Web hosting is the most expensive option, but can be cost-effective if you anticipate high-volume Web traffic and are looking for a customized solution with good customer service and support.

Each of these solutions meets different business needs and provides varying levels of control and service. The difference in cost can be considerable, however, so it might take you a while to find the right balance between what you need and how much you are willing to pay.

When choosing a Web host provider for your site, the key features to consider include the following:

- Disk space
- Connection speed and transfer bandwidth
- Stability and security
- Flexibility
- Uptime
- Customer service and support

> Verify which features are included in the 'standard' Web space assigned to you. Some providers charge extra for email accounts, for example.

Disk space

Many Web host providers charge a flat rate for a fixed amount of **disk space** (also known as **Web space**). You can then purchase additional space if you require it.

If your site is fairly small with limited graphics and video content, you'll probably find that 50 megabytes (MB) of disk space is more than sufficient (and in this case, your free Web space may well be sufficient). If your site is particularly rich in graphics and video content, or contains a lot of file downloads, then you'll need more space—consider 100 to 300 MB.

To determine the total size of your Web site

- In Windows Explorer, right click on the folder containing your Web site and click **Properties**.

  The **Properties** dialog displays the total size of the site, and also how many files and folders it comprises.

Connection speed and transfer bandwidth

These terms can be confusing, especially to the novice Web site designer, but they all relate to your customers' experience as they interact with the pages of your Web site.

- The term **connection speed** is generally used to refer to the amount of data your viewers can access on your site, in a given time period. The faster the connection speed, the faster your viewers will be able to click through pages, view images and video clips, download files, and so on.

If you choose shared hosting, your customers will be competing with customers of the co-hosted sites for access to the Web server. During peak periods, this may result in slower response times, or even "Web Site Not Responding" messages.

> The average Web site requires between 100 and 1500 MB of transfer bandwidth.
>
> Most Web host provider packages include tools to help you monitor your Web site's transfer bandwidth usage.
>
> In WebPlus, the **Resource Manager** includes tools to help you determine the size of your Web pages, and track down items that might make them too large.

- **Transfer bandwidth** refers to the amount of data that your viewers can download over a certain time period— this amount may be fixed and limited, as specified in the contract between you and your Web host provider. Thus, the transfer bandwidth you will need is directly related to the number of visitors you anticipate, and the size and content of your Web site.

If your site is mainly comprised of text and is light on graphics, you'll need less transfer bandwidth. Graphics, video, and other multimedia files use up more transfer bandwidth, and some providers may limit downloads for these file types. For example, they may restrict image and video file downloads to 50% of your site's allotted transfer bandwidth.

You can usually exceed your transfer bandwidth limit, but your provider will charge you for this.

As a rule, dedicated and managed Web host packages have higher transfer bandwidth allowances—worth keeping in mind if you have a particularly large or dynamic Web site, or anticipate extremely high volumes of traffic.

To calculate your transfer bandwidth requirements

- Use the following formula to calculate an approximate transfer bandwidth for your site:

  Average page size (including graphics and multimedia files) x number of page views x 30 days

  For example, suppose you have an average page size of 12 KB, plus 50 KB of graphics, and you anticipate that every day, 20 people will visit your site and will view an average of 5 pages per visit. Your formula would look like this:

  (12 + 50) x (20 x 5) x 30

  62 x 100 x 30 = 186,000 kilobytes (or 186 MB of transfer bandwidth each month)

Stability and security

It's important that you research the Web hosts you are interested in.

Ask friends and colleagues for recommendations, read reviews in magazines and online. You should be confident that the provider you choose is successful and not likely to go out of business. Check that they have been in operation for at least a few years—you can usually find this information on the 'About' page of the provider's Web site.

A reliable Web host provider with a good track record will also be committed to maintaining and upgrading the hardware and software required to run their operation successfully. They should also be able to answer questions about how they secure their Web servers, and how often they upgrade firewall and security software.

Flexibility

Your Web site may initially be small, but what if your product line expands, your customer base grows, and business explodes? If you started off with a 'beginner' hosting package, it's likely that this no longer meet your needs.

Your provider's services should be flexible and scalable so that they can change and expand along with your business. Most shared providers allow you try a variety of features, without forcing you to commit for a long period. You can then adjust and upgrade as required.

Uptime

The term **uptime** refers to the percentage of time that a Web site is 'available' for visitors to access. Ideally, we'd all like our Web sites to be accessible 24 hours a day, 7 days a week, but from time to time, all Web host providers will need to take their Web servers offline to conduct routine maintenance and upgrades. Many providers boast 99% uptime, but good ones will back this up with uptime records, and will include an uptime guarantee in your contract (they may also offer a refund or price reduction if this is not met).

Customer service and technical support

When you sign up with a Web host provider, you're buying more than just space and bandwidth for your Web site, you're buying a service. You want to be sure that if you need help, you can get it quickly and easily, for a reasonable cost.

Generally, the more support you require, the higher the price. Most shared and managed providers offer round-the-clock support. Some hosts advertise free customer support, but what exactly does this mean? Ask about hours of operation and the type of support that is provided. For example, is it via email only or telephone? If by telephone, at what rate? What's the average waiting time?

Setting up email accounts

Most Web host provider packages will provide a certain number of mailboxes and email 'aliases' for your Web site. For example, most companies use different email addresses for their sales, customer service, and technical support departments.

Even if you are a very small company, we suggest you do the same as multiple email addresses will add credibility to your business.

Optimizing for search engines

You've spent time and money developing an enticing Web site, but that doesn't necessarily mean that you'll attract visitors.

Search Engine Optimization (SEO) refers to the process of increasing the volume of traffic to a Web site by improving its ranking in browser search engine results.

This is an important subject, and we've devoted an entire tutorial to it! See "Optimizing Your Site for Search Engines" for tips on a wide range of SEO strategies including meta tags, keywords, page properties, ALT text and TITLE tags, search engine submissions, and more.

In this document, we've highlighted the main steps involved in setting up a Web site for commercial use. We hope you've found it useful and informative, and are now feeling better equipped to get your own business up and running on the Web.

For more information, and hands-on exercises, on creating business Web sites, see the other titles in the **Creating Business Web Sites** tutorials section.

Creating an E-Commerce Web Site

The Web site we created in the "Adding Dynamic Content to Your Web Site" tutorial has received great feedback and the photographer now wants to sell his prints online. He has asked us to add e-commerce functionality to the site and, fortunately for us, WebPlus includes all the tools we need.

In this project, you'll learn how to:

- Sign up with an e-commerce shopping cart provider.

  In this project, we'll use PayPal© as our shopping cart provider. You may decide to use a different provider, depending on your needs and the product(s) you want to sell on your site.

- Add an e-commerce form and button to your site.

This tutorial assumes that you have completed the "Creating Personal Web Sites: Adding Dynamic Content to Your Web Site" tutorial. If you haven't worked through this exercise, you can apply the procedures described to your own Web site, or create a new one.

In the following sections, we'll add new pages and iFrames to our photography Web site, set up and configure a shopping cart provider, and insert and configure an e-commerce form.

1: Setting up the new pages and iFrame

Before we add the e-commerce functionality to our Web site, we're going to replace our existing **Collection** page with a **Purchase** page.

Currently, the **Collection** page contains a poll (Smart object) and a photo gallery. We'll replace these objects with a set of thumbnails of the photographs offered for sale, and an inline Frame (iFrame).

The content of the iFrame will be dynamic, linking to pages (one for each thumbnail) displaying a full-size version of the selected thumbnail, along with an e-commerce form showing the particular purchasing options for this photograph.

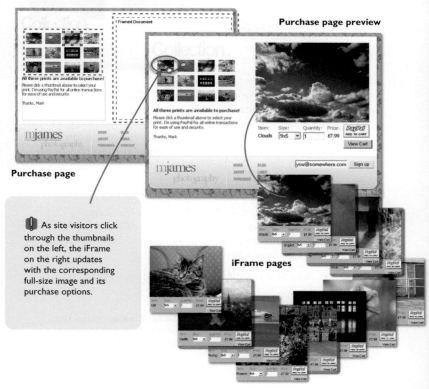

Purchase page preview

Purchase page

iFrame pages

As site visitors click through the thumbnails on the left, the iFrame on the right updates with the corresponding full-size image and its purchase options.

Constructing our **Purchase** page may sound complicated, but the actual process is really quite simple. For this exercise, we'll assume you worked through the "Adding Dynamic Content to Your Web Site" tutorial, and that your photo gallery site resembles ours.

1   Open your photo gallery Web site, or the site to which you want to add e-commerce functionality. (If you worked through the previous project and have created a site containing Smart objects, we suggest you make a copy by saving it under a different filename.)

2   On the **Site** tab, click ⊞ **Add** to add a new page. In the **Insert** dialog, accept the default settings and click OK.

    Click on the page (labelled Page 7 by default) and drag it down to the bottom of page list.

3   Right-click the new page and click **Page Properties**.

4   In the **Page Properties** dialog:

    • Change the **Page name** to 1.

    • Click **Change**, change the file name to **1.html** and click **OK**.

    • Change the **Master page** to **(none)**.

    • Click **OK**.

5   Working on the new page, click 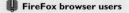 **Import Picture** and import the first image you want to list for sale. Place the image in the top left corner of the page and resize it so that it's about 308 pixels wide by 220 pixels high—you can check this on the **Transform** tab.

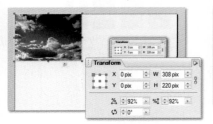

> 🔔 **FireFox browser users**
>
> If you're using FireFox as your browser, you need to left-align your image to ensure that it displays in the upper-left section of the iFrame.

We've finished with this page for now, but we'll return to it later to add our **e-commerce** form.

6   If you completed the previous project, "Adding Dynamic Content to Your Site," open the **Collection** page in the workspace and delete the poll and the photo gallery objects. Alternatively, on the **Site** tab, add another new page to your site.

7   Right-click the page and select **Page Properties**. In the **Page Properties** dialog:

- Set the **Page name** to **Purchase**.

- Click **Change**, change the file name to **purchase.html** and click **OK**.

- Set the **Master page** to **Master A** and click **OK**.

8   Open the **Master A** page in the workspace.

On the navbar, select the Collection button and click the 〔 T 〕 **Edit Theme Graphic** button. In the **Theme Graphic Settings** dialog, change the button text to 'PURCHASE' and click **OK**.

Let's add the thumbnails and iFrame to our page.

9   Open the **Purchase** page. Use the ▨ **Import Picture** tool to import all of the images you want to list for sale.

10 Position your images as a thumbnail 'gallery,' sizing them appropriately (each of our images is 45 by 32 pixels).

The image you imported on to your page **1** should be the first thumbnail in the gallery.

Use the **Align** tab to precisely align your images.

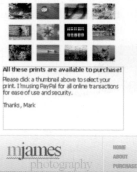

11 Click the ▦ **HTML Frame** tool and insert a text frame beneath your thumbnails. Use this to add any relevant information and/or instructions for your site visitors.

Now lets add our iFrame.

12 On the Web Objects toolbar, click the ▭ **Framed Document** tool and then click and drag to create a large frame on the right of your **Purchase** page. (Ours is 333 pixels wide by 300 pixels high).

13 When you've created your iFrame, once you release the mouse button, the **Hyperlinks** dialog opens by default. We will now link our iFrame to the new page (named **1**) we created in steps 2 to 4.

14 In the **Framed Document** dialog:

- Select the **Site Page** option.

- In the **Page name** drop-down list, select **1**.

- If you want users to be able to bookmark to the image frame, select the **Export as absolute URL** check box; otherwise leave this unchecked.

- In the **Scroll Bars** list, select **No**.

- Click **OK**.

We've just linked our iFrame to the page showing the full-size version of our first thumbnail. Now, when visitors first view the **Purchase** page, this image will be displayed in the frame.

Our next task is to link the image thumbnail to the **1** page—so that when visitors click on the thumbnail, the full-size image will display in the iFrame.

15 Right-click the matching image thumbnail and select **Hyperlink**. In the **Hyperlinks** dialog:

- Select **Site Page**.

- In the **Page name** drop-down list, select **I**.

- In the **Type** drop-down list, select **Document Frame**, and check that **ifrm_I** is selected in the corresponding list.

- Click **OK**.

Note: You won't be able to see the effect of this step until you've linked the other thumbnails. We'll do this later, but first we need to finish our **I** page by adding the e-commerce functionality.

Once this is complete, we can use the page as a template to create pages for all the other thumbnails.

We've set up the basic structure of our pages. Next, we'll configure our shopping cart provider and then add an e-commerce form to our page.

2: Choosing a Shopping Cart Provider

You've made the decision to sell your products over the Internet and have created a site that will attract your target market.

But how do you accept and process payments from your customers?

> Some providers offer additional features and depending on your needs, these may or may not be important to you.
>
> Use the provider's Web Help pages to find out more about unique shopping cart features.

Any Web site that supports e-commerce activity will typically make use of a shopping cart system and a payment processing system. If you've ever bought anything online, you will already be familiar with this concept.

There are many third-party shopping cart providers that can be used. Each provider offers the same basic features—product catalogue, 'running' customer basket, 'buy it now' option, secure payment information capture and checkout, and so on.

With WebPlus, you can choose one of our selected providers, all of which offer a good range of features.

In this project, we've chosen PayPal© as the provider most suited to sell our prints. We'll now step you through the signup and configuration process.

To setup and configure a PayPal shopping cart

1 On the Web Objects toolbar, on the E-Commerce flyout, click the 🖳 **Configure E-Commerce** button.

2 In the **E-Commerce Configuration** dialog, select the **PayPal** option and choose one of the following options:

- If you already have a PayPal account, click **Next**.

- If you don't have an account, click **Sign Up Now**. The PayPal site opens in your browser. Follow the instructions provided to register and set up an account. When you have finished, return to WebPlus.

3 In the **PayPal Configuration** dialog, type the email address where you want to receive notification about payments received.

Optional step (recommended): If you want to use PayPal's **Sandbox**, a test tool for trying out your shopping cart before going live, select this option.

To use the Sandbox, you must set up a separate test account (in addition to your live PayPal login) through PayPal's Developer Central site. Click **Find Out More** to do this.

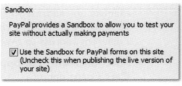

Sandbox

PayPal provides a Sandbox to allow you to test your site without actually making payments

☑ Use the Sandbox for PayPal forms on this site (Uncheck this when publishing the live version of your site)

4 Click **Finish**.

Once you've configured your shopping cart, you're ready to insert an e-commerce object.

3: Inserting e-commerce objects

WebPlus provides Wizards to help you create e-commerce objects by completing a series of dialogs.

You can add your e-commerce objects as a form or link, depending on the characteristics of the item(s) you are selling.

> For information on the differences between forms and links and why you might choose one over the other, see "Inserting an e-commerce object" in online Help.

In our example, we'll add a form since it offers more flexibility and allows for some user interactivity.

To insert a PayPal form

1 Open your **I** page in the workspace.

2 On the Web Objects toolbar, on the E-Commerce flyout, click the
   Insert an E-Commerce object button.

3 In the **Add PayPal Object** dialog:

   • Select the email address which is to receive the payment information.

   WebPlus assumes that the email address set during shopping cart configuration is used. If you want to use a different address—for

   example, the address you specified when you set up your Sandbox, clear the **Use the site default address** box and select a different address to override the site default.

   • Select the **Add to Shopping Cart Form** option.

   • Click **Next**.

4 In the **Button Image** dialog:

   • Select the **Use a standard image** option.

- Select the image of your choice—we chose the first one.
- Ensure that the **Embed image file in site** option is selected.
- Click **Next**.

5 In the **Item Details** dialog, enter the following information:

- **Item Name:** The name of the item for sale. We typed 'Clouds'—the title of the photograph displayed on our page 1. Try to make this descriptive as it will appear as the item description on the invoice produced by the cart.

- **Item ID:** If you have a specific product code reference, enter it here. We left ours blank.

- **Currency:** Choose the currency required from the drop-down list.

- **Price:** Type the price of the item.

- Click **Next**.

6 The **Item Description** can be used to add extra details about the sale item.

As we already have an image, we don't need to add another. However, you might want to add a more detailed description of the item.

Click **Next.**

7 We want customers to be able to choose between several different print sizes, so in the **Item Options** dialog:

- Select **Add an options field**.

- In the **Name** box, type 'Size.'

- In the **Prompt** box, type 'Size:'

- Select the **Combo Box** option.

- Click **Add Option**...

For information on the other options in the **Item Details** and **Item Options** dialogs, see online Help.

8 In the **Combo Box Option** dialog:

- In the **Name** box, type '9x5 inches.'

- In the **Value** box, type '9x5 inches.'

- Click the **Selected** check box— to designate this as the default option that is automatically selected when the page opens.

- Click **Add Another**.

9 Repeat step 8 to create a '12x8' option, this time do not select the **Selected** check box.

10 Repeat step 9 to create a '24x16' option and then click **OK**.

Your **Item Options** dialog should now list the three options you specified, as illustrated left.

11 Click **Next**.

12 The **Item Options** dialog displays again, allowing you to add a second options field. We don't want to do this so click **Next**.

13 In the **Item Details** dialog:

- Select the **Add Edit Box** option to let the customer define the quantity to be ordered.

- In the **Shipping and Handling** section, type the charges associated with the order.

- If left blank, the default profile will be used.

- Click **Next**.

14 In the **Extra Customer Information** dialog, in the **Customer Address Information** drop-down list, select **Customer prompted for address**.

Click **Next**.

15 In the **Payment Pages** dialog, leave the default settings and click **Next**.

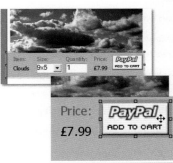

16 In the **Form Layout** dialog, leave the default settings and click **Finish**.

17 Click and drag on your page to insert the e-commerce form on your page, beneath the imported image.

If necessary, you can move the individual form objects, and edit their appearance, as you would any other WebPlus object.

18 Click on the PayPal logo button and drag it up to the top of the form, making a space beneath it.

We're now going to insert another e-commerce object into the space created—a **View Shopping Cart** button.

To insert a PayPal button

1 On the Web Objects toolbar, click the 💲 **Insert an E-Commerce** object button.

2 In the **Add PayPal Object** dialog:

- Select the email address you used previously.

- Select the **View Shopping Cart Link** option.

- Click **Next**.

3 In the **Button Image** dialog:

- Select the **Use a standard image** option.

- Select the image you want to use.

- Click **Finish**.

4 Click to insert your button at default size, then drag it into position on your form.

5 Preview your page in your Web browser. Check that you can:

- Select a **Size** from the drop-down list.

- Edit the product **Quantity**.

- Add items to your shopping cart.

- View your shopping cart.

If you're happy with the way your first product page looks and functions, you can use it as a template for your other pages by simply copying and editing it.

We'll do this next...

To copy and edit a Web page

1   On the **Site** tab, right-click page **I** and select **Insert Page....**

2   In the **Insert** dialog, do the following:

- In the **Page name** box, type '2.'

- In the **Master page** drop-down list, select **(none)**.

- Select the **Copy objects from page** check box and ensure that **1** is selected in the adjacent drop-down list.

- In the **Placement** section, select the **After** option and ensure that **1** is selected in the adjacent drop-down list.

- Click **OK**.

A new page, **2**, is added to the **Site** tab.

3   Open this page in the workspace. You'll see that it is an identical copy of **1**, containing the same image and e-commerce objects.

4   Right-click the image and select **Replace Picture** (or click the 🖼 **Replace Picture** icon).

5 In the **Import Picture** dialog, browse to locate the second image you want to sell on your Web site. Select the file and click **Open**.

Now we need to edit the e-commerce form to match this new item.

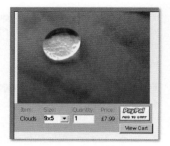

6 Right-click the e-commerce form and select **Edit E-Commerce Form**.

7 In the **Add PayPal Object** dialog, click **Next**.

8 In the **Button Image** dialog, click **Next**.

9 In the **Items Details** dialog, check the details displayed and replace any that do not apply to your new item.

(In our case, we only needed to type in the name the new image displayed on page **2**.)

Click **Next**.

10 In the **Item Options** dialog, replace any of the options that have changed for this new item. If the same options apply, as in our case, simply click **Next** to proceed.

11 Click **Next** (unless you want to add another option for this item).

12 In the **Item Details** dialog, edit the shipping and handling charges if required. If no changes are required, click **Next**.

In steps 4 and 5 of this section, we used the WebPlus 'Replace Picture' command, which simply replaces one image with another inside the same sized frame.

For this to be successful, the new image must be the same size as the original.

In our example, we used Serif PhotoPlus to resize our images before importing them into WebPlus.

13 In the **Extra Customer Information** dialog, click **Next**.

14 In the **Payment Pages** dialog, click **Finish**.

15 WebPlus asks you if you want to reformat the form, click **No** (if you choose **Yes**, the PayPal button will be moved back to its original default position in the lower right corner of the form).

> In our sample photography site, we only need to change the name of each item as all other options (for example, print size and price) stay the same.
>
> When you create your own e-commerce site, the extent of the changes required in these dialogs will depend on the type of items you are listing for sale.
>
> If your items are very different, you may prefer to simply create each page from scratch, rather than copying and editing your first page as we have done here.

16 Open the **Purchase** page in the workspace. Right-click the second image thumbnail and choose **Hyperlink**.

17 In the **Hyperlinks** dialog:

- Select the **A page in your site** option.

- In the **Page name** drop-down list, select **2**.

- In the **Type** drop-down list, select **Document Frame**, and then check that **ifrm_1** is selected in the corresponding list.

- Click **OK**.

18 Preview the **Purchase** page in your browser.

Click on the second thumbnail to display the corresponding full-size image and purchase options on the right.

Now that you have two pages in place, it's easy to add the rest of your product pages.

19 Simply repeat the previous steps to insert a new page for each image thumbnail, replacing the image and editing the e-commerce form as required.

20 When you've added all of your pages, preview and test your e-commerce site in your Web browser.

Your finished **Purchase** page should look something like ours.

Congratulations, you've created your first e-commerce Web site! We hope you've enjoyed the exercise and wish you every success in your e-commerce ventures.

If you also worked through the "Creating a Personal Web Site" and "Adding Dynamic Content to Your Site" tutorials, you should by now be feeling very comfortable with WebPlus tools and well-equipped to start working on your own WebPlus creations—whether their purpose is personal or for profit!

🔍 Search Engine Optimization

To learn about how you can attract visitors to your site (so that they can start purchasing those products!), see the "Creating Business Web Sites: Optimizing Your Site for Search Engines" tutorial.

Adding a Forum to Your Site

Use the new forum Smart object to host interactive discussions on your Web sites.

In this tutorial you'll learn how to:

- Create a Serif Web Resources account.

- Set up access control.

- Create a forum—on a page of your Web site, or as an offsite link.

- Configure, manage, and edit user groups and forums.

- Sign up and post to a forum.

- Add a forum moderator group.

- Create and edit forum user ranks.

- Suspend and block IP addresses and users.

> If you are a new WebPlus user, or haven't worked with Smart objects before, we suggest you take a look at the "Creating Personal Web Sites: Adding Dynamic Content to Your Site" tutorial before beginning this one.

Adding a Forum to Your Site

A forum allows visitors to your Web site to interact, hold discussions, and 'post' general comments and questions. Not only do forums allow you to gather feedback from the people who visit your site, they also provide a place for visitors to go to learn more about your products and services, or to discuss a common topic of interest.

WebPlus provides a range of interactive and dynamic objects (including forums, blogs, hit counters, and polls), all of which 'collect' user information. These objects are known as **Smart object**s and are available from Serif Web Resources, a secure online service which not only hosts the objects, but also stores the associated data on secure server space designated to Serif.

1: Setting up a Serif Web Resources account

To access the Smart objects, you need to log in to Serif Web Resources. If you don't have a valid username and password you must first create a Serif Web Resources account.

To create a Serif Web Resources Account

1   On the Web Objects toolbar, click the 🌸 **Smart Object** tool.

2   In the **Serif Web Resources** login dialog, click **Create Account**.

3   In the next dialog:

   • Type your email address.

   • Type your password twice.

   • Click **Signup**.

4   If the address specified is not already associated with a Serif account, an additional dialog asks you to complete some personal details.

5   A confirmation email is sent to your email address. Click the link in the email and you're ready to access Serif Web Resources!

> 📘 **Creating a Serif Web Resources account**
>
> If your email address is known to Serif (you've previously registered), you'll be asked a few questions to complete registration.
>
> If your email address is unknown to Serif (you're new to Serif or unregistered), you must complete full security. Follow the instructions on the login screens.

To access Serif Web Resources

1 On the Web Objects toolbar, click the 🌸 **Smart Object** tool.

2 In the login dialog:

- Type your username (email address).

- Type your password.

- **Optional:** To access Serif Web Resources directly in future, bypassing the login screen, select **Remember account details**.

- Click **Login**.

The **Smart Objects** dialog opens.

Note that Smart objects are not added directly to the page from Serif Web Resources, but are first added to an object library displayed in the left **My Smart Objects** pane.

The Smart Objects Library lets you manage and edit your objects and add them to your Web pages immediately or later.

If you have not created any Smart objects prior to this tutorial, the library will be empty.

2: Setting up access control

Before you can create a forum, you first need to set up access control.

Access control lets you apply security across your site (typically to specific pages of your site). In this exercise, we'll set up access control to allow users to enter a forum by logging in to an **Access Control** Smart object.

The following steps show you how to add the forum and login control to a page of your Web site, or as an offsite link.

To set up access control

1   If you want to add your forum and user login to a page of your site, open the page in the workspace. (If you want to set up your forum as on offsite link, it doesn't matter which page is open.)

2   Click the 🏵 **Smart Object** tool and log in to Serif Web Resources.

3   In the **Smart Objects** dialog, click **New**.

4   In the **Create Smart Object** dialog, select the **Access Control** option and click **OK**.

5   In the **Create New Access Control** dialog, name your Access Control object.

- If you want to create an on-the-page user login, set the properties of the text, buttons, background, and border.

- If you want to create your forum as an offsite link, ignore these settings.

6   Click **Create**. Your new Smart object is listed in the Smart objects Library.

7   To create an on-page user login control, click **Insert**, and then click on your page to insert the object at default size.

- or -

If you want to create your forum as an offsite link, click **Exit** to log out of Serif Web Resources.

> 🛈 This tutorial focuses on forums, but you can use access control to apply security to other pages of your site, such as those containing confidential information. How you apply access control depends on the complexity and nature of your Web site. For more details, see online Help.

3: Creating a forum

Now that you have set up access control, you can create your forum.

To create a forum

1 In the **Smart Objects** dialog, click **New**.

2 In the **Create Smart Object** dialog, select the **Forum object** and click **OK**.

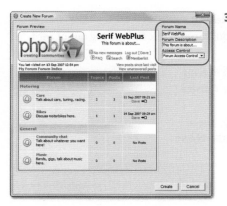

3 In the **Create New Forum** dialog:

- Name your forum.

- Type a brief description of the forum.

- In the **Access Control** drop-down list, select the Access Control object you created in the previous section.

- Click **Create**.

Your forum is added to the Smart objects Library and ready to be added to your site—either on a page of your site, or as an offsite link.

To add a forum to a page of your site

1   With the forum selected in the
    Smart objects Library, click **Insert**.

2   Click and drag on your page to set
    the size of the object.

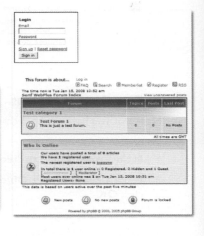

> 💡 If your Smart objects do not preview
> on the page, you can turn previews back
> on:
>
> 1   Click **Tools**, then **Options**.
>
> 2   In the **Options** dialog, select **UI
>   Settings** and then select the **Smart
>   Object Previews** check box.

To add a forum as an offsite link

1   Once you have created your forum, click **Exit** to log out of Serif
    Web Resources.

2   On the **Site** tab, in the ⊞ ▾ **Add**
    drop-down list, click **New Offsite
    Link**.

3   In the **Offsite Link** dialog, select
    Smart Object and click the **None**
    button.

4   In the Smart Objects
    Library, select your
    forum and click **Select**.

5   Name your forum menu
    item, choose a target
    window, and select the
    Include in Navigation
    check box.

6   Click **OK**.

The offsite link is added to the **Site** tab.

On your Web page, a new button is added to the navbar.

4: Configuring access control

When we set up access control, a default user group was automatically created for this object. The next task is to configure access control so that when a visitor signs in, they are also automatically added to the user group and logged into the forum.

To configure access control

1 Click the 🌼 **Smart Object** tool and log in to Serif Web Resources.

2 In the Smart Objects Library, select your **Access Control** object.

In the **Object Preview** pane, click **Manage**.

3 In the **Manage Access Control** dialog, under **User Group Management**, the **Group** drop-down list displays the name of your forum group.

You will also see that your email address was added to the user group when you set up access control.

• Click the **Manage Group** button.

The **Group Management** panel displays the properties of the group.

4 Leave the **Add new
   users on signup** check
   box selected.

   - If you are adding your
     forum to a page of
     your site, select
     **Automatic
     login/logout**.

   Your site visitors will
   now be logged in to the forum when they log in to the access
   control, even if the forum is on a different page.

   - or -

   For an offsite link, leave the **Automatic login/logout** check box
   clear. Site visitors will be able to log in directly on your offsite
   forum, and will not need to navigate away from them.

   - Click **Update Group** and then click **Done**.
   - Click **Exit**.

5: Configuring and managing the forum

You have now created everything you need to get your forum up and
running. However, there are a few configuration tasks you should know
about before you go 'live' with your site.

If you take a look at the preview of your forum Smart object, you'll see
the first main section is titled 'Test category 1,' with 'Test Forum 1'
listed beneath it. These are the default settings that are automatically
added to every new forum.

Each Forum object can have multiple categories, each of which can also
have multiple 'subforums.'

The **Manage Forum** dialog lets you edit the default test category and its subforum, and create additional categories and subforums.

You can also edit forum and subforum descriptions, add a moderator group, set permissions, change the style (theme) of the forum, add and rank users, and set user permissions.

> 🛈 **Setting forum permissions**
>
> The **Manage Forum** dialog also includes a **Forum Privacy** section. Here, you can set permissions to determine if non-registered visitors to your site can read your forums.
>
> - If you want non-registered visitors to be able to read your forums, set permissions to **Publicly readable**.
>
> - If you only want registered visitors to view your forums, set permissions to **Private**.

In the next section, we'll do the following:

- Edit the default category and its subforum.

- Add a new forum to the updated category.

- Add a second category and subforum.

- Change the forum theme.

To edit the default category and subforum

1   In the Smart Objects Library, select your forum and then in the **Object Preview** pane, click **Manage**.

2   In the **Manage Forum** dialog, in the **Forum Management** section, replace the default **Category Name** text with your own category name.

Click **Update Category**.

3   Type your new **Forum Name** and **Forum Description**.

Click **Update Forum**.

Forum Management

To edit the name of a category or forum, change its old name and press enter, or press es

Category Name
Working with Forums   Update Category

Forum Name   Forum Description
Adding categories   Issues related to adding forum categories

                           Moderated By Group
                           No moderation ▾

To add a new subforum to an existing category

1   In the **Add New Forum** section, type a name and description for your new subforum.

2   In the **Forum Category** drop-down list, select the category to which you want to add the new subforum (you will only see one category listed.)

> Add New Forum:
>
> Forum Name | Forum Description
> Adding subforums | Issues related to adding subforums to categories
>
> Forum Category
> Working with Forums ▾ | Add Forum

3   Click **Add Forum**.

4   Scroll back to the **Forum Management** section to see your updated category name with its two subforums listed beneath it.

> **Forum Management**
> To edit the name of a category or forum, change its old name an
>
> Category Name
> Working with Forums | Update Category
>
> Forum Name | Forum Description
> Adding categories | Issues related to adding forum c
> | Moderated By Group
> | No moderation ▾
>
> Forum Name | Forum Description
> Adding subforums | Issues related to adding subforu
> | Moderated By Group
> | No moderation ▾

Let's now add a second category and subforum to our main forum.

To add a new category and subforum

1   In the **Add New Category** section, type the name for your new category and click **Add Category**.

> Add New Category:
>
> Category Name
> Using site tools | Add Category

2   In the **Add New Forum** section, type a name and description for your new subforum.

3   In the **Forum Category** drop-down list, you'll now see two categories listed. Select the new category you created in the previous step.

> Add New Forum:
>
> Forum Name | Forum Description
> Resource Manager | Issues related to using the Resource Manager
>
> Forum Category
> Using site tools ▾ | Add Forum
> Working with Forums
> Using site tools
> New category added successfully.

4   Click **Add Forum**.

In the **Forum Management** section, you will see your new category and its subforum listed beneath it.

Finally, let's change the general appearance of the main Forum object by applying a different theme.

To change a forum theme

1   In the **Manage Forum** dialog, in the **Forum Themes** section, select a theme from the drop-down list and then click **Update Theme**.

2   Click **Exit** to close the **Manage Forum** dialog and return to the **Smart Objects** dialog.

3   Click **Exit** to return to the WebPlus workspace and preview your forum.

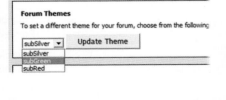

With your Access Control and Forum Smart objects configured, you're now ready to see how they work together.

6: Signing in to access control and posting to the forum

You'll now assume the role of a visitor to your Web site. You'll sign in to access control and then post a new topic to the forum.

For this section, use a different email account to the one you used to sign up for Serif Web Resources. If you don't have an alternate email address, it's very easy to set one up (you can create free email accounts at Yahoo, Hotmail, AOL, and many other providers' sites).

To sign in to the Access Control object

1   On the Standard toolbar, in the 🔍 ▾ **HTML Preview** drop-down list, click **Preview Site in <your browser>**.

2   If you have placed your forum and Access Control objects on a page of your site, click the **Sign up** hyperlink in the **Login** dialog.

- or -

If you have used an offsite link, click the relevant navbar button, and then click **Register** at the top of the forum page.

3   Your browser is redirected to a **Forum Account - Sign up** page.

Complete the details as requested and then click **Signup**.

The email address you specified on the Signup page will receive an email with the subject **Account Activation (Forum Account)**.

4   Click the link in the email to activate your account.

5 Return to your Web page. In the **Login** dialog, type your email address and password, and this time click the **Sign In** button. The dialog updates to show that you are logged in and provides options to log out, change your password, and change your screenname.

- or -

If you have used an offsite link, click **Login** at the top of the forum page.

6 Click on a subforum, and then click the **Post new topic** button.

7 Type your subject and message body into the text boxes and then click **Submit**.

You can now choose to view your message or return to the **Forum Index** page, which now indicates that a post has been created.

7: Adding a moderator group

The forum moderator is the person, or group, who monitors the forum—usually on a daily basis. The moderator's role is to prevent forum users from posting offensive messages, or messages that are not related to the forum topic.

Moderators can edit and delete posts, and also delete, lock, unlock, split, and move topics in the forum. You can take on this role yourself, or you can assign someone else the position. Either way, if you want to assign a moderator to your forum, you will need to do the following:

- Create a new group.

- Add a user to the group.

- Assign the group to the forum Smart object.

- Designate the group as the forum moderator.

To create and assign a moderator group

1 Log in to Serif Web Resources.

2 In the Smart Objects Library, select your Access Control object.

   In the **Object Preview** pane, click **Manage**.

3 In the **Manage Access Control** dialog, under **Create New Group**:

   - In the **Group Name** text box, type a name for your moderator group.

   - In the **Group Smart Object** drop-down list, select your forum Smart object.

   - Do not select the **Add new users on signup** check box.

   - If you are adding your forum to a page of your site, you can also select **Automatic login/logout**.

     For an offsite link, leave this check box clear.

   - Click **Create Group**.

- Click **Done** to return to the **Manage Access Control** dialog.

You can now add users to your Moderator group.

4   In the **User Group Management** section:

- In the **Group** drop-down list, select the Forum Moderator group.
- In the **Users** list, click a user.

  Because you signed up to the forum as a new user with an alternate email address, you will see two users in this list.

- Click **Add** to add the selected user to the Moderator group.

- Click **Manage Group**.

The **Manage Access Control** dialog displays your updated group properties and user.

- Click **Done**.

- In the **Smart Objects Library**, select your Forum object and click **Manage**.

5 In the **Manage Forum** dialog, under **Forum Management**:

- Locate the subforum to which you want to add a moderator.

- In the **Moderated By Group** drop-down list, select your forum moderator group.

- Click **Update Forum**.

- Click **Exit** to close the Smart Object Library.

When your site is published to the Web, members of the moderator group will be able to click a link (located in the lower right corner of the subforum and topic pages) to open the **Moderator Control Panel**.

In the **Moderator Control Panel**, the moderator can delete, move, lock, unlock, and split forum topics.

You **can** post new topics in this forum
You **can** reply to topics in this forum
You **can** edit your posts in this forum
You **can** delete your posts in this forum
You **can** vote in polls in this forum
You **can** moderate this forum

8: Creating, editing, and assigning user ranks

A **rank** is a title that appears in each user's profile, and next to their screenname when they post to a forum.

You can use ranks to indicate something about a member or group of members. For example, to indicate that certain users have a special status, or to show how active they are on the forum, and so on.

There are two types of ranks, **normal ranks** and **special ranks**.

- Normal ranks are granted to all users based on their forum post count.

- Special ranks are granted to specific users in the **Rank User** section of the dialog.

To create a new normal rank

1   In the **Manage Forum** dialog, scroll to the **User Rank Management** section.

2   In the **Add New Rank** section, in the **Rank Title** box, type a name for the new rank.

Add New Rank

Rank Title		Min. Posts	Special Rank
Power User		100	☐

Add Rank

3   In the **Min. Posts** box, type the minimum number of posts users must have created in order to achieve this rank.

For example, in our illustration, a user would be granted the **Power User**

Edit Ranks

Rank Title	Min. Posts	Special Rank		
Site Admin		☑	Update Rank	Delete Rank
Power User	100	☐	Update Rank	Delete Rank

rank only after creating 100 forum posts.

4   Click **Add Rank**.

The new rank is added to the rank list.

To create a new special rank

1 In the **Manage Forum** dialog, scroll to the **User Rank Management** section.

2 In the **Add New Rank** section, in the **Rank Title** box, type the name for the new rank.

3 Leave the **Min. Posts** box empty and select the **Special Rank** check box.

4 Click **Add Rank**.

To assign a special rank to a user

In the **Rank User** section:

- Select a user from the first drop-down list .

- Select the special rank from the second drop-down list.

- Click **Set Rank**.

9: Editing Smart objects

Once an Access Control or forum (or any Smart object) has been created, you can edit it in the Smart Object Library or directly on the page.

Editing an Access Control object allows you to change the appearance (text, colour, and so on) of the Login dialog; editing a Forum object allows you to change the forum description only.

Once you have created a forum, you cannot change its main forum name, or the Access Control object associated with it.

To edit a Smart object

1 On the Web page, right-click the Smart object you want to edit, and then click **Edit Smart Object**.

2 Make your edits as required and then click **Save**.

10: Suspending and banning users

In addition to ranking your users, you also need to protect your forum from unwanted users.

In the **Manage Access Control** dialog, the **User Control** section allows you to suspend users temporarily for breaking site rules (for example, for posting defamatory statements on a hosted public forums).

If more drastic action is required, a user's IP address can be banned from accessing the forum. As a last resort, even the ISP or organization to which the owner of the email address belongs can be banned.

As a general rule, the latter option is not recommended. However, it may sometimes be necessary to prevent institutional malpractice such as professional spamming.

> Banning an ISP or organization can result in innocent visitors to your site also being banned. It is recommended that you only apply an ISP ban as a last measure.
>
> Note that banning a single ISP from America Online may also affect other users.

To suspend a user

1   Log in to Serif Web Resources.

2   In the Smart Objects Library, select your Access Control object, then in the **Object Preview** pane, click **Manage**.

3   In the **Manage Access Control** dialog, under **User Control**, select a user from the **Email** drop-down list.

4   Click **Suspend User**.

In the **Manage Access Control** dialog **Users** list, suspended users are indicated with an asterisk.

The next time the user tries to log on, the message "Your account has been suspended" is displayed.

To reactivate a suspended user

- Select the user and click **Unsuspend User**.

To ban a user by IP address

1 Follow steps 1 to 2 of the previous section, 'To suspend a user'.

2 In the **Ban User's** drop-down list, select **IP address**.

3 Click **Ban**.

To ban a user by ISP or organization

1 Follow steps 1 to 2 of the previous section, 'To suspend a user'.

2 Click the **Lookup User** button.

   Serif Web Resources locates the user's ISP/organization network address and displays it in the scrolling window.

3 In the **Ban User's** drop-down list, select **ISP/organization**.

4 Click **Ban**.

If a user's IP address, ISP, or organization is banned, it is listed in an **Unban** drop-down list. The entry will also include the date the address was banned.

> As the **Lookup User** function relies upon external Web sites (those responsible for allocating IP addresses), it may sometimes fail due to timing out.

This allows you to review current bans and reverse them if the user, IP address, or organization is no longer considered suspect.

In this tutorial, we've shown you how to set up access control for a forum. However, don't forget that access control can also be used to restrict access to other areas of your site—download pages, contact lists, and so on. For more information, see online Help.

Adding an Image Catalogue

In this tutorial, we'll use WebPlus X2's new **database merge** functionality to showcase a collection of artwork.

You'll learn how to:

- Create a photo database.
- Insert a repeating area on the page.
- Open and edit a database.
- Add hyperlinks providing site visitors with access to additional information about a record.
- Merge and publish data.

Adding an Image Catalogue

In this exercise we'll create an image catalogue for a graphic artist's Web site. We'll create a photo data source from a folder of images, and merge the data into a repeating area on our page. We'll then customize the repeating area, and edit the data to create an attractive catalogue of artwork samples. We'll complete the following steps:

- Create a photo database from a folder of images.

- Insert repeating areas for the data.

- Insert placeholders into repeating areas.

> The Photo Data Source function handles image files in any standard format.

- Open and edit the database.

- Merge and publish the data.

- Link summary and main pages for each record, using anchors and hyperlinks.

- Link merged page names to image and HTML file names.

1: Preparing the site

In preparation for inserting our image catalogue, we did the following:

1 We created a 🗋 new blank site, adding a banner and company details to the top of the master page.

2 On the **Site** tab, we added a ⊞ new blank page and named it **Draft layout**.

3 On our **Draft layout** page, we created a mockup of the page layout we wanted to achieve.

(You can do this in WebPlus, or with paper and pencil.)

If you create your draft layout in WebPlus, you'll need to either delete this page before you publish your site, or clear its check box in the **Publish to Web** dialog (see section 7, "Merging and publishing the site," step 5.).

2: Creating the database

We're now ready to create our photo database. You can use a collection of any images for this exercise, but before completing the following steps, you'll need to save all of the images to the same folder on your computer.

To create a photo database

1 On the **View** toolbar, select **Toolbars**, then click **Database Merge**. (This toolbar is hidden by default.)

2 On the **Database Merge** toolbar, click ⁺🗀 **Create photo database**.

3 In the **Photo Data Source Wizard**, click **Browse**, then locate the source folder containing the images you want to database. (All images must be contained in the same folder.) Select the folder and click **OK**.

4 Click **Next**.

5 If required, edit the file name of the database to be created, or accept the default name.

Click **Next**.

6 The Wizard displays a list of image files found in the designated source folder.

Initially, all images are checked for inclusion in the database. If required, you can clear check boxes to exclude specific images.

Click **Next**.

7 The Wizard displays a list of Exif data fields that may be associated with your images.

In this exercise, we don't want to include this information so click **Select None** to clear all of the check boxes.

8 Click **Finish**.

WebPlus builds the database, and displays the data in a rows and columns in the **Merge List** dialog.

Here, you can customize the data to be merged by including or excluding specific records, filtering the records, or editing the data.

> 💡 Keen photographers may find the Exif data useful: Each database record created will consist of a path name for the photo, plus fields containing additional Exif data (date and time, equipment, software, etc.) that may have been automatically stored with the original file.

9 In the **Merge List** dialog, click **Edit**.

The **Edit Database** dialog displays the details of the first record in the database.

Click in the **Path Name** field to see a thumbnail preview of the image associated with this record.

10 In the **View Records** section, scroll through the records by clicking the arrow buttons.

We'll return to the **Edit Database** dialog later, when we edit our database.

For now, click **OK** to close the dialog.

11 Click **OK** to close the **Merge List** dialog.

3: Creating the repeating area

Now that we have created our photo database, we can associate it with a **repeating area** on a Web page. Inside this repeating area, we can then insert our database picture and text fields, along with any other elements that we want to repeat on the page (in this case, a shape).

To create the repeating area

1 On the Database toolbar, click ⊞ **Insert Repeating Area**.

2 In the **Choose merge database** dialog, click **Browse**, then browse to and select the database created in the previous section.

3 Click **OK**.

The **Repeating Area Tile Setup** dialog lets you choose the layout required for your page.

Position

Left: 0 pix
Top: 0 pix

Size

Width: 250 pix
Height: 250 pix

Gaps

Gap X: 0 pix
Gap Y: 0 pix

Layout

Across: 3
Down: 4

☐ Extend page to fit all tiles

OK   Cancel   Help

Referring back to our **Draft layout** page, we want to display our images in a 3 column x 4 row grid.

To do this, in the lower-right **Layout** section, set the **Across** value to 3 and the **Down** value to 4.

4   Click **OK** to close the dialog.

🗓 Setting up the repeating area

You can set precise properties for the repeating area in the dialog, or close the dialog and then click and drag to set the repeating area's size and shape directly on the page.

5 On your page, WebPlus creates a placeholder for the first cell of the repeating area.

If required, you can:

- Move the repeating area cell by clicking and dragging it.

- Resize the repeating area cell by dragging its border handles.

We can now add the objects that we want to display in each repeating area on the page. We'll start by creating a simple QuickShape, which we'll use as a 'frame' for each image.

6 On the ☐ ▾ QuickShapes flyout, click the **QuickRectangle** and then click and drag on the page to create a rectangle. Drag the left node down to round the corners.

- On the **Swatches** tab, apply a white fill.

- On the **Line** tab, in the line style drop-down list, select **None**.

7 On the ☐ ▾ Effects flyout, click *fx* **Filter Effects**.

In the **Filter Effects** dialog, select the drop shadow check box and then set the following values:

Opacity 36; **Blur** 3.75; **Distance** 3.75; **Angle** 135

Click **OK**.

8 Drag the rectangle into the repeating area, resizing it so that it just fits inside.

Now let's add our database fields to the repeating area.

9 On the Database Merge toolbar, click 📷 **Insert Picture Field**.

10 In the **Insert Picture Field** dialog, in the **Fields** list, you'll see **Path Name** selected by default. Click **Insert** to insert this field, and then click **Close**.

WebPlus adds the **{MM:Path Name}** placeholder to your page at default size.

11 Drag the placeholder into the repeating area and resize it so that it fits inside the rectangle shape. Leave some space underneath to add the image title.

4: Editing the database

Next, we'll edit our database, creating additional text fields for the image titles and descriptions.

To edit the data source

1 On your Web page, click to select the border of the repeating area placeholder (make sure you select the repeating area itself and not the **{MM:Path Name}** placeholder).

On the Database Merge toolbar, click 📷 **Edit Database**. (You can also click **Edit Database** on the context toolbar.)

2 In the **Choose merge database** dialog, your database file name is displayed in the **Data source** text box. Click **Edit**.

3 In the **Edit Database** dialog, click in the **Path Name** field to see a thumbnail preview of the image associated with the record.

Click **Customize**.

4 In the **Customize Database** dialog, click **Insert**.

5 In the **Field Name** dialog, type "Image Name" and click **OK**.

6 Repeat steps 4 and 5 to add a second text field. Name this field "Description."

7 Click **OK** to close the **Customize Database** dialog.

In the **Edit Database** dialog, your new fields are added to the record details.

8 Type the name and description of your first image directly into the text boxes, then click the right arrow button to move to the next record.

9 Repeat step 8 to add names and descriptions for the remaining images, then click **OK** to close the dialog.

10 Click **OK** to close the **Choose merge database** dialog.

11 On the Database Merge toolbar, click 🏛 **Insert Text Field**.

In the **Insert Text Field** dialog, in the **Fields** list, select **Image Name**.

12 Click **Insert** to insert this field, and then click **Close**.

WebPlus adds the **{MM:Image Name}** placeholder to your page at default size.

13 Drag this new placeholder into position under the image placeholder.

Centre align the text by clicking ≡ **Align Centre** on the Text context toolbar.

14 Click 💾 **Save** to save your work.

5: Merging data into the repeating area

Now that we have selected which records to merge (that is, we have created our **merge list**), and inserted our placeholders, we're ready to merge the database content to a temporary Web site and preview the results of our work.

To merge the repeating area

1 On the Database Merge toolbar, click 🖼 **Merge to New Site** (or click 🖼 Merge to New Site on the context toolbar).

WebPlus generates a new Web site (adding the suffix '**_merge1**' to the file name) in a separate window, replicating the repeating area as many times as there are records in the database, and replacing the placeholders with the relevant database fields.

The layout uses the grid arrangement you specified (3 x 4 in our example), with each unique cell including data from a single record, following the order of records in the merge list.

> In our example, all of our 12 records fit on a single page. However, WebPlus will insert new pages as needed to include all records in the database.

2 **Optional:** To adjust display properties such as picture scaling and alignment for any individual picture frame, right-click the frame and click **Frame Properties...**

Note that the original Web site remains open in its own window. Don't forget to save it in case you need to repeat the merge process with another data set!

If you're not happy with the resulting merged Web site, return to the original site, make adjustments, and repeat the merge process.

3 When you're happy with your page layout, close the merged site window and return to your original site.

6: Adding a details page, anchor, and hyperlink

In this final section, we'll add some interactivity to our site. We want site visitors to be able to click on an image thumbnail to open a new page containing a larger version of the image, and a detailed description.

To add the details page

1 On the **Site** tab, click **Add** ⊞ to add a new blank page to your site. In the **Insert** dialog, accept the default page settings for now.

2 On the Database toolbar, click ⊡ **Insert Repeating Area**.

3 In the **Choose merge database** dialog, click **Browse**. Select your image database and click **OK**.

4 In the **Repeating Area Tile Setup** dialog, choose a 1 column x 1 row grid layout. Click **OK**.

5 Resize the repeating area so that it fills your page.

6 Copy the QuickRectangle from your Home page, and then paste the shape onto your new page.

7 Resize the shape and position it at the top of the repeating area. Leave enough space at the bottom of the page for the Description text field.

8 On the Database Merge toolbar, click **Insert Picture Field**.

9 In the **Insert Picture Field** dialog, click **Insert** to add the **Path Name** field, and then click **Close**.

10 Drag the **{MM:Path Name}** placeholder into the repeating area, resizing it so that it fits inside the rectangle. Leave some space underneath to add the image title.

11 On the Database Merge toolbar, click **Insert Text Field**.

12 In the **Insert Text Field** dialog, select **Image Name**, click **Insert**, and then click **Close**.

Drag the **{MM:Image Name}** placeholder into position under the image placeholder.

13 Repeat step 10 to add the
{MM:Description} placeholder to
the bottom of the page.

14 Select each text field placeholder in
turn, and then use the controls on
the Text context toolbar to apply
formatting as required.

For example, for our Description
field, we applied 10 pt Verdana, and
left-aligned the text.

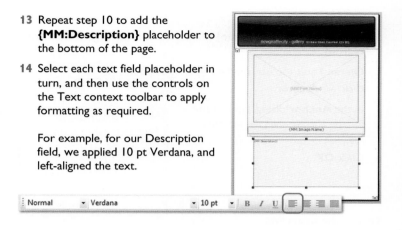

15 On the **Site** tab, right-click your new page and click **Page
Properties**.

- In the **Page Properties**
dialog, to the right of the
Page name text box,
click ▤ **Insert Merge
Field**.

- In the **Insert Text Field**
dialog, select **Image
Name** and click **Insert**.

On the **Site** tab, you'll see
the page name is updated
with the **{MM:Image
Name}** placeholder text.
(You'll see why we did this
when we merge the data.)

We've finished placing the required elements into our repeating areas.
Now all we have to do is link the thumbnail images on the Home page
to the larger images and descriptions on the **{MM:Image Name}** page.
We'll use an anchor and a hyperlink for this.

To add the anchor

1 On the **{MM:Image Name}** site page, select the large **{MM:Path Name}** placeholder.

2 On the Tools toolbar, on the Hyperlinks flyout, click ⚓ **Anchor**.

3 In the **Anchor** dialog, type a name for the anchor—we named ours BigPic.

4 Click **OK**.

To add the hyperlink

1 Open the Home page in the workspace and select the thumbnail **{MM:Path Name}** placeholder.

2 On the Tools toolbar, on the Hyperlinks flyout, click 🔗 **Hyperlink**.

3 In the **Hyperlinks** dialog, in the left tree view, click **Anchor**.

4 To the right of the list, in the **Anchor** section of the dialog:

   • In the **Page name** drop-down list, select the **{MM:Image Name}** page.

   • In the **Anchor** list, select the anchor you created in the previous section.

   • In the database record drop-down link, select **Same record as origin of link**.

5 Click **OK**.

6 Save your file.

When you save a Web site, WebPlus 'remembers' the current data source and reopens it automatically the next time you open the site—so as long as you're using the same source, you won't need to reopen it yourself.

7: Merging and publishing the site

Our site is finished, but before we can publish it, we need to repeat the merge process to include the changes we have made to our database and site structure.

To merge and publish the data

1   On the Database Merge toolbar, click
    Merge to New Site (or click
    Merge to New Site on the context toolbar).

    WebPlus generates a new Web site (adding the
    suffix '_merge2' to the file name) in a separate
    window, creating a {MM:Image Name} page
    for each record in the database.

    You'll see these pages listed on the **Site** tab.

    You'll also see that WebPlus has replaced the
    page name placeholder text with the text found
    in each **Image Name** field. If we had not
    replaced the default page name with the
    {MM:Image Name} placeholder, all of these
    pages would have been named Page 3.

2   Double-click on one of your generated pages to preview it.

3   **Optional**: To adjust picture scaling and alignment for any individual
    picture frame, right-click the frame and click **Frame Properties...**

    When you're happy with your page layout, you're ready to publish
    your Web site.

4   On the Standard toolbar, click 🖫 **Publish to Disk**, or 🖫 **Publish
    to Web**.

5   In the **Publish** dialog, select all the pages of your site, except for the
    Draft Layout page created in section 1, "Preparing the site."

6   Choose your publishing options as required, and then click **OK**.

7   View your site in your Web browser.

8   Click on an image thumbnail to open the details page for that record.

> For details on the choosing your publishing options, see the online Help or the "Getting Started: Previewing and Publishing Your Site" tutorial.

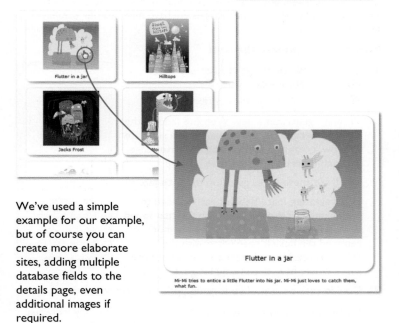

Flutter in a jar

Mi-Mi tries to entice a little Flutter into his jar. Mi-Mi just loves to catch them, what fun.

We've used a simple example for our example, but of course you can create more elaborate sites, adding multiple database fields to the details page, even additional images if required.

Note also that WebPlus X2 lets you present other types of content—product lists, contact lists, e-commerce data, and so on, from a variety of data sources. For more details, see online Help.

Optimizing Your Site for Search Engines

Previous tutorials have shown that some consideration at the design stage can help to make your site easier to navigate, easier to read and understand, and more Web-friendly. In this exercise, we'll show you how to make your site 'search engine-friendly.' The following topics will be discussed:

- Meta tags, keywords, and keyword analysis.
- Planning content and copywriting.
- Page properties and Web export options.
- Image ALT and TITLE tags.
- Hyperlinks and anchors.
- Site descriptions.
- Search engine file generation—sitemap.xml and robots.txt.
- Search engine submissions and fees.
- Spider simulators.
- Link building and analysis.
- Consultancy services and resources.

Optimizing Your Site for Search Engines

You've spent time, money, and effort developing an enticing Web site, but that doesn't necessarily mean that you'll attract visitors. On the other hand, improving your site's ranking in search engine results will definitely get you noticed!

This tutorial offers a number of tips and search engine optimization (SEO) strategies.

Web site keywords

Keywords can be individual words or whole phrases. They can appear almost anywhere, even hidden in the HTML code as a **meta tag** or **keyword tag**.

We'll start with this meta tag and then progress to more significant design considerations.

1 Create a new, blank Web site by clicking
   📄 **New**, or by clicking **Create > Start New Site** in the Startup Wizard.

2 On the **File** menu, choose **Site Properties...** and then click the **Search** tab.

3 Enter your choice of keywords in the lower text box. Separate your keywords and keyword phrases with commas. For example, sculpture, stainless steel sculpture, dragon sculpture, stainless-steel.

   Click **OK** when you're done.

Multi-page sites

The site-wide keywords you enter will be included on each page of your site.

If you have a multi-page site and certain pages offer unique content, you can supplement the keyword and description information on a page-by-page basis.

To set keywords for a page

1 Click **Edit**, then **Page Properties**. Click the **Search** tab and type in your keywords. Click **OK**.

    Having page-specific keywords and descriptions that better match the body text on each page will help improve your site's chances of a higher search engine ranking.

2 Click the arrow on the 🔍▾ **HTML Preview** button to expand the drop-down menu. Choose to preview this page in your browser of choice.

3 In your browser, choose to 'View Source' (usually available from the browser's **View** menu).

    Notice where your keywords have been added in the HTML code. Page-specific or site-wide keywords and descriptions all appear in the same place in the HTML code.

> \<title\>Home\</title\>
>
> \<meta **name**="keywords" **content**="keyword, keywords, search engine optimization, search engine optimisation, google search results, copywriting, internet marketing, keyword, keywords, search engine optimization, search engine optimisation, google search results, copywriting, internet marketing"\>
>
> \<meta **name**="description" **content**="Improve your Internet marketing strategy, increase your search result ranking, choose great keywords, optimize your site for Google and much more."\>

As you can see from our coloured HTML snippet, the keywords are stored in a meta tag—a named piece of information within the HTML code—called 'keywords.'

The site description is also stored in a meta tag (called 'description'). These specific 'tags' are created in the **Site** and **Page Properties** dialogs, but thanks to WebPlus you don't really need to worry about the HTML code or how meta tags are generated; it's all taken care of for you!

Choosing keywords

When choosing keywords, think about your site, its content, any products or services you are offering, and your site's target audience. It may help to know what keywords people are actually searching with, as well as thinking about what you offer in particular.

For example, you might find you are competing with millions of other sites if your searched-for keyword is 'sculpture' but only a couple of thousand of other sites if your searched-for keyword is 'stainless steel sculpture.'

If you offer information, products, or services for new parents, don't forget that 'pregnant' and 'pregnancy' are amongst relevant keyword terms, too.

Write down your choice of keywords and use a thesaurus to identify similar words. Consider abbreviations or longer versions of words, as well as different word forms and plurals. Note common misspellings and variations of your chosen words (UK and US English versions for example).

Do some online research. For example, type "good keywords" into your search engine and you'll find a wealth of information to help you.

You can also consider using free or paid-for services and software to extend your ability to choose the best keywords for your site.

Additional research will give you the benefit of seeing which keywords are most commonly used in search terms; this will help you reach either a wider market with popular terms or a niche market with less-competitive terms.

Having carefully chosen a set of keywords, you need to know some important tips about how else they can be used.

Once your site is published, the meta keywords are stored hidden from view in your HTML source code. But the *visible* text carries more weight when a search engine decides how to rank your site. Many search engines, including Google™, do not use meta tag keywords in their search engine technology, so you'll need to go beyond the WebPlus Site and Page Properties dialogs. Let's explore this further...

> ❗ Keywords and other search engine related tweaks can also be accessed via the 🗂 Site Manager . For more information about either the Site Manager or assigning keywords to your site, see online Help.

Body text (copywriting)

The main **body text** or **copy** of each page is crucial. Writing engaging content is the first stop for improving search results! Make sure your chosen keywords are well represented in the body text. If your site's keywords cover stainless steel sculpture, for instance, it would be wise for those exact words to appear in your body text.

In addition to writing finer detail in your copy, you should also include broader descriptions and terms frequently. You may also like to include keywords in your copy text with bold or italicized formatting, and give them prominence in your first body text paragraph, as these attributes may lead to those words being given more prominence in search rankings.

It's not difficult to write copy with the keywords in mind, and it's far more attractive and effective for those words to be included in your main copywriting than cheekily added as a list somewhere on the page.

Using your keywords in your main copy can also make up for any key terms used on buttons or menus that are published as graphics—search engine 'spiders' (discussed later) can't read any text that has been converted to a picture. Giving careful consideration to keywords in copy text is always recommended; however, it may only impact search engine rankings for less competitive search terms.

Again, we suggest you do some research on the subject. There are ranges of books dedicated to copywriting—even copywriting specifically for Internet search engine optimization. Try searching on "SEO copywriting."

Page title

The name of each page of your site appears throughout WebPlus and helps you to manage and identify your pages. This page name normally becomes the **title** and is stored both in the hidden published HTML code, and in the visible title bar of viewers' Web browsers.

If you want the public to see a page title other than the default WebPlus page name, you can specify an **HTML title** on the **Page** tab of the **Page Properties** dialog.

Your choice of page title will be a factor in search engine optimization, sitting between the copy text and filename in importance.

File name

Each page you create in your WebPlus site has a title (as mentioned previously) and a **file name**—which is what Web browsers look for if directed to a folder rather than to a specific page.

For instance, by default the published file name for the first page is usually **index.html**. For all other pages you have total freedom in choosing the published HTML filename.

Again, you can set the file name on the **Page** tab of the **Page Properties** dialog.

Hyperlinks and anchor names

You can use navigation bars to help your site's visitors find their way from page to page, but you should also consider some text-based hyperlinks to other pages on your site and to important sections of long pages (which you can mark with anchors).

The hyperlink and anchor names, as well as words either side of them in the copy, are analyzed by search engine technologies and will add weight to your content's credibility.

For more information on hyperlinks and anchors, see the "Getting Started: Creating Hyperlinks" tutorial.

HTML tags

HTML text frames offer you the ability to design with HTML-compliant styles. This means that you can format text in your HTML frame using heading styles from H1, H2, ..., to H6. These styles are applied to the entire paragraph.

An advantage of this is that text applied with <Hn> styles are given priority over <P> styles (the default) in Internet search engines, with the <H1> tag being given highest priority.

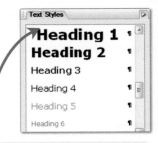

To apply an HTML meta tag

1   Select the HTML frame to change all of the text or select only the relevant paragraph.

2   Click or hover over the ⊦ handle (near the Web Objects toolbar) to display the **Text Styles** tab.

3   Select ☑ Show All to see all of the text style options.

4   Click on "Heading1" to apply the H1 tag, "Heading 2" for the H2 tag and so on.

🔲 The **Text Styles** tab contains preset Heading styles which translate to HTML tags H1 to H6. You can format the text style to suit your site design whilst keeping those important tags. For more information on modifying text styles see online Help.

Image ALT and TITLE tags

It's possible to add some HTML text tags to your imported images (and other objects that will be published as images).

The text can be entered on the **Alt and Title** tab of the **Image Export Options** dialog, available on an object's right-click menu.

- TITLE text is the tooltip text that will appear when site visitors hover over the image in their Web browsers. This text is often used when clicking on a image has some function, for example, opening a larger version of the image in a new window.

- ALT text, used to describe the content and/or purpose of an image, is the text that will appear in the area of your page where the image will download. (Note that ALT text should *not* be used for images whose only purpose is decorative.)

By default, the **Use default ALT text** option is selected. This tells WebPlus to use the TITLE text as the ALT description so that you only have to enter it once.

Using pertinent keywords for these text strings adds further weight to your site's content.

Q You can create ALT text without adding TITLE text, or use a different ALT text description by clearing the **Use default ALT text** option.

Site description

The site description, as entered in the **Site Properties** dialog or the **Page Properties** dialog, can be used by search engines to help determine a rank for your site amongst search results.

Aim to have a clear, concise description containing many of your chosen keywords and keyword phrases.

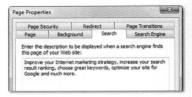

Let's now consider what happens once your site is finished and published—how will search engines find it?

Some search engine companies accept submissions of sites for inclusion in their search results, while others use automated systems (often called **spiders**) to find and help rank sites. These electronic arachnids follow links to your site from known resources (or find your site in the search engine's own directory) and analyze your site's keywords as well as other content. You can rely on spiders to find your site if you wish, or submit your site for inclusion in a search engine's listings, sometimes at a price.

Search engine file generation—sitemap.xml and robots.txt

By default, each published page will have all of its content indexed—the information is automatically collected by the search engines—and Heading text is given a priority. However, to help compete with the billions of other pages also being indexed, it is worth giving this process a helping hand. There are two files that WebPlus can generate which should help search engines to accurately index your site—sitemap.xml and robots.txt.

Sitemap.xml

Web crawlers discover pages from links within the site. Sitemap.xml supplements this data and allows crawlers to pick up all of the URLs. Essentially, sitemap.xml is a list of all of the pages that you really want indexing and provides extra information about

> Don't get confused between sitemap.xml and the navigation Sitemap. Although they have similar names, sitemap.xml is a search engine tool only. A navigation Sitemap is a collection of hyperlinks that acts like a dynamic table of contents.

each URL, such as how often the page changes, when it was last updated, how important it is compared to the other site pages... All of this information can really improve your site rankings. So, what if you can't write in XML? No need to worry, WebPlus takes care of it for you.

To create a sitemap file

1 On the **File** menu, click **Site Properties...** and choose the **Search Engine** tab.

2 Select the **Create search engine sitemap file** option (it is recommended that you do not change the filename).

3 Select **Index pages on this site** and choose which **Sitemap Settings** you wish to apply.

4 If you want to display page priority, it's worth remembering that 0.0 is the lowest and 1.0 is the highest setting.

5 Click **OK**.

Individual pages on the site can be given different settings to the rest of the site, or be entirely excluded from the sitemap file.

1 Right click on the relevant page in the **Site** tab and choose **Page Properties...** In the dialog, click on the **Search Engine** tab.

2 Check the **Override site search engine settings**.

3 Once you have finished making your changes, click **OK**.

Robots.txt

Whereas sitemap.xml tells the Web crawler to index the page and follow its links, robots.txt does the opposite. Essentially, it provides a list of pages that should not be indexed. This can be useful if you do not want to include one or more links that go to external sites. Robots.txt generally works in conjunction with the robots meta tags for more precise settings. For more information, see online Help.

To create a robots.txt file

1   On the **File** menu, click **Site Properties...** and click the **Search Engine** tab.

2   Select the **Create search engine robots file (robots.txt)** check box.

3   Click **OK**.

For the overall site properties, it is best to leave the **Index pages on this site** option selected. If you have a page that you do not want to index, you can do this from the **Site Manager** dialog.

1   Open the **Site Manager** by clicking 🔲 Site Manager on the Pages Context toolbar.

2   Under **Page Properties**, click on **Search Engine**.

3   Ensure **Override Site** is checked for the page that you do not want to index.

4   Uncheck **Index Page**.

5   When you have finished, click **Close**.

Search engine submissions

You should definitely try to get your site listed in the free **Open Directory Project**, www.dmoz.org.

The Open Directory Project is a totally free online directory used heavily by other search engine companies, so getting listed there will help make your site appear in a greater number of search results.

Submitting your site to the Open Directory and having it approved by one of the volunteer staff may take some time, perhaps months, but is worth the effort. Be aware that your site may be rejected for the following reasons:

- If there is no unique content.
- If the content is illegal.
- If your site is under construction.
- If you have suggested an inappropriate category for your submission.
- If you have used an automated submission program or service.
- If your description is not accurate, concise, or is too 'promotional' in nature.
- If your site is already listed.

Choosing the right keywords before publishing and applying for inclusion on the Open Directory is likely to prove more effective than submitting your site to multiple search engines at length—although you do need to be listed somewhere first to get the process in motion!

Take care to try and get your site's description right first time—the Open Directory volunteer staff are so busy that an edit to your entry may be unachievable.

Keyword analysis

Keyword Density Analysis (again, you can search online for this term) may shed further light on the success of your site in search engine results. You can use special software or online services to compare the frequency with which a keyword occurs in comparison with one of your competitors—choose a competitor with high-ranking search results for a worthwhile comparison.

The analysis often differentiates between words in titles, image tags, copy text, hyperlinks, the domain name, and of course official 'meta tag keywords.' This information will help determine if you can improve on the current frequency and usage of keywords.

Search engines may favour a site against its competitors because of a higher density of keywords in the copy text and other areas.

Spider simulators

Keywords and how to use them obviously feature very highly in Web site design. We've tried to 'see with the eyes of our visitors,' while thinking about keywords and how people search... now let's see 'through the eyes of an Internet spider'!

There are some applications and Web sites that offer a view of your own Web site comparable to that of a search engine spider. A spider's-eye-view of your site might help you determine if you have made good use of keywords.

For example, consider Google's approach by viewing your site through a text-only Web browser such as the Lynx browser. A range of spider simulators can be found with an Internet search (try "spider simulator").

While the above tips will make your site search-engine-friendly, you may find that full optimization is required if your desired search terms are already very popular on the Web. If you have thought about keywords, their use in different ways, and have checked your site's suitability for search engines by using a spider simulator, what else can you do? There are lots of doors open to you; we'll discuss a few of them now...

Fees and payment

As mentioned, you can submit your site to search engines and directories (sometimes at a cost), additionally you can pay a service fee to have guaranteed frequent 'spidering' so your entry with a search engine is updated regularly. You can also consider using 'pay-per-click' advertising such as Google's AdWords™.

Link building

You should make efforts to build links, to get other sites to link to yours—preferably reputable sites with content relevant to your own—and look at some niche directories. Avoid signing up to 'link farms,' sites that focus purely on offering links to other sites that are irrelevant to their own content, as these may be ignored by search engine companies (your site ranking may even be harmed by association).

Some links to your site will carry more weight or relevance when a search engine ranks your site. A site's Google Page Rank™, for instance, can be ascertained by installing the 'Google Toolbar™' (http://toolbar.google.com/index_xp.html).

You should aim to have links to your site on other relevant sites that already have a respectable Google Page Rank (5 or higher). Sites with a high Page Rank are 'spidered' more often, so your site in turn will be found and spidered more often if you have links from such respectable sites.

These link-building methods will increase the chances of your site being included in more search engine results, while the relevance of links and the content (use of keywords) will contribute to your ranking.

Link analysis

You can also consider **link analysis** services or software—tools which will analyze successful sites and report on their optimization methods.

As you move forward with the evolution of your online presence, you may want to know detailed information about your visitors' habits—if and when they leave your site, how they found your site and much more.

Web trackers and analysis software and services abound; your Internet Service Provider or Web host may be able to offer basic information as part of your hosting package, or you could consider external services.

External services are often able to offer a far greater level of accuracy and detail (for instance, at a basic level just differentiating between unique and repeat visitors is a great distinction). Of course last but by no means least, you can learn from professionals with an expertise in search engine optimization and search engine marketing (SEM).

Consultancy

Although the Internet is new to many people, some are already seasoned experts and have grown up with finding ways to improve their (and others') use of the Internet. Whether you wish to use paid services or not, you should examine some consultancy services and resources for advice, further learning, and often guaranteed better results.

That concludes our list of search engine optimization tips. We hope you'll find them useful when planning and constructing your own Web sites.

Web Site & Email Templates

Web Site Templates

WebPlus X2 provides you with a selection of Web site design templates that you can use as starting points for your own sites. These are available from the **Program CD** and **Resource CD**, and were designed using theme graphics and Smart objects making them fully customizable. The following categories are included:

- Business
- E-Commerce
- Entertainment
- Interest
- Personal

Email Templates

Also included are a collection of email templates. These are grouped into two categories: Business and Home. Again, these templates are fully customizable—whatever the occasion, it has never been easier to share your news!

To access the templates:

1 From the **Startup Wizard**, select **Create** > **Use Design Template**.

2 In the **Create New Site from Template** dialog:

- Browse to and select the template you want to use.

- Choose a **Button Theme** and **Scheme** from the drop-down lists.

- In the **Pages** pane, choose the pages to include by selecting their check boxes, (they are all selected by default.)

- Click **Open**.

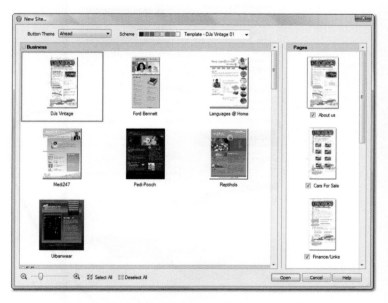

You'll find a wide range of additional design templates in the Serif WebPlus X2 Template Packs—**Business & Commerce** and **Home & Hobby**.

For more details, see the Serif Web site.

Djs Vintage

About us

You can adopt the functionality used in the templates such as this contact form.

For more information on adding forms to your Web sites, please see the tutorial **Creating a Personal Web Site**.

Cars For Sale

Finance & Links

Services

Shows

Terms of Use

Privacy Policy

Blank Page

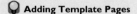

💡 Adding Template Pages

If you click ⊞ ▼ **Add** on the **Site** tab and choose **New Blank Page**, WebPlus inserts a blank page based on your existing template into your site.

Alternatively, choose **New Template Page...** to open the **Add New Page From Template** dialog, which allows you to preview and choose an existing or new blank page.

Ford Bennett

Home

Welcome

Finance
Volutpat. Integer fringilla. Duis lobortis, quam non volutpat suscipit, magna sem consequat libero, ac hendrerit urna ante id mi. Quisque commodo facilisis tellus.

Litigation
Integer sodales lorem sed nisl. Morbi consectetuer mauris quis odio. Ut dolor lorem, viverra vitae, viverra eu, euismod nec, enim. Lorem ipsum dolor sit amet, consectetuer adipiscing elit.

Commercial
Morbi nisl eros, dignissim nec, malesuada et, convallis quis, augue. Vestibulum ante ipsum primis in faucibus orci luctus et ultrices posuere cubilia Curae; Proin aliquam, leo at luctus tempus, augue. Fusce in nisl vitae massa venenatis rhoncus. Praesent orci velit, lobortis eget, suscipit semper.

Corporate
Volutpat. Integer fringilla. Duis lobortis, quam non volutpat suscipit, magna sem consequat libero, ac hendrerit urna ante id mi. Quisque commodo facilisis tellus.

Real Estate
Integer sodales lorem sed nisl. Morbi consectetuer mauris quis odio. Ut dolor lorem, viverra vitae, viverra eu, euismod nec, enim. Lorem ipsum dolor sit amet, consectetuer adipiscing elit.

Integer sodales lorem sed nisl. Morbi consectetuer mauris quis odio. Ut dolor lorem, viverra vitae, viverra eu, euismod nec, enim. Lorem ipsum dolor sit amet, consectetuer adipiscing elit.

Finance
Volutpat. Integer fringilla. Duis lobortis, quam non volutpat suscipit, magna sem consequat libero, ac hendrerit urna ante id mi. Quisque commodo facilisis tellus.

Litigation
Integer sodales lorem sed nisl. Morbi consectetuer mauris quis odio. Ut dolor lorem, viverra vitae, viverra eu, euismod nec, enim. Lorem ipsum dolor sit amet, consectetuer adipiscing elit.

Commercial
Morbi nisl eros, dignissim nec, malesuada et, convallis quis, augue. Vestibulum ante ipsum primis in faucibus orci luctus et ultrices posuere cubilia Curae; Proin aliquam, leo at luctus tempus, augue. Fusce in nisl vitae massa venenatis rhoncus. Praesent orci velit, lobortis eget, suscipit semper.

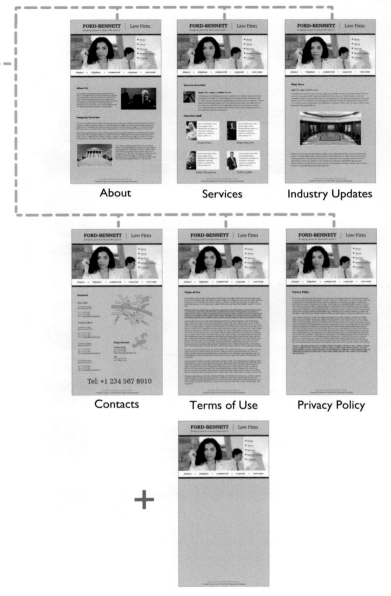

About

Services

Industry Updates

Contacts

Terms of Use

Privacy Policy

Tel: +1 234 567 8910

+

Blank Page

Languages @ Home

Home

You can adopt the functionality used in the templates. For example, comments or contact forms can be directed to your own email address.

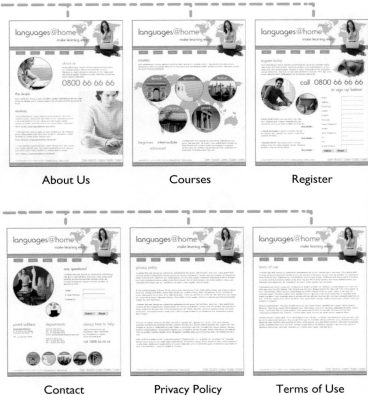

About Us

Courses

Register

Contact

Privacy Policy

Terms of Use

Blank Page

Medi247

Company Info

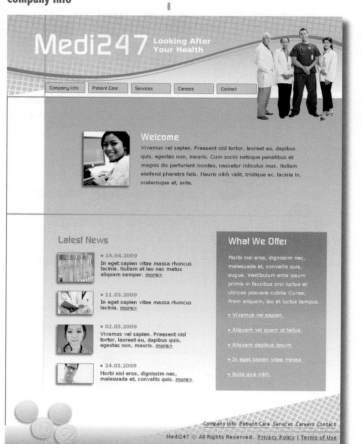

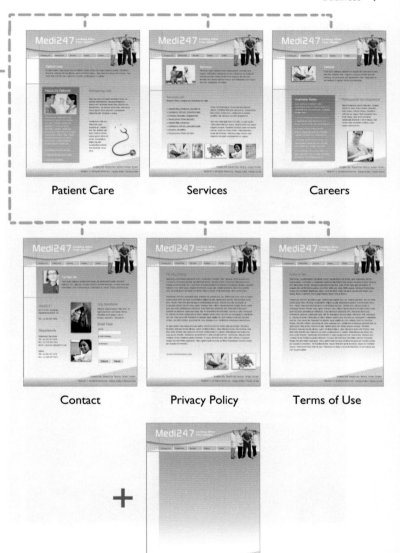

Patient Care

Services

Careers

Contact

Privacy Policy

Terms of Use

Blank Page

Pedi-Pooch

Home

Welcome

Pellentesque tincidunt, dolor eu dignissim mollis, justo sapien iaculis pede, vel tincidunt lacus nisl sit amet metus. Fusce ac est vitae purus varius tristique, sociosqu ad litora torquent per conubia nostra.

About us

Morbi pellentesque, mauris interdum porta tincidunt, neque orci molestie mauris, vitae iaculis dolor felis at nunc. Maecenas eu diam a leo porta interdum. In non massa quis odio feugiat sagittis. Quisque ac lorem. Maecenas ut sem sed ipsum suscipit malesuada. Nulla quis dui quis.

Book an appointment now

FREE first consultation
1 (234) 5678 910

Metus ac quam donec

In hac habitasse platea dictumst. Mauris rutrum enim vitae mauris. Proin mattis eleifend pede. Sed pretium ante sit amet elit. Quisque pede tellus, dictum eget, dapibus ac, sodales dictum.

Award Winning Service

)) **Aliquam dapibus ipsum vitae sem.** Ut eget mauris ac nunc luctus ornare. Morbi pellentesque, mauris.

more

"In eget sapien vitae massa rhoncus lacinia. Nullam at leo nec metus aliquam semper". Phasellus tincidunt, ante nec lacinia ultrices, quam mi dictum libero, vitae bibendum turpis elit ut lectus. Sed diam ante, lobortis sed, dignissim sit amet, condimentum in, sapien. Pellentesque nec lectus non risus auctor lobortis. Vestibulum sit amet dolor a ante suscipit pulvinar. Sed lacinia.

News update...

In eget sapien vitae massa rhoncus lacinia, est vitae purus varius tristique, sociosqu ad litora torquent per conubia nostra.

more

HOME   HEALTH & BEAUTY   TRAINING   POOCH HOTEL   CONTACT US

Health & Beauty

Training

Pooch Hotel

Contact Us

Privacy Policy

Terms of Use

Blank Page

Reptihols

Gallery

For more information on adding Flash photo galleries to your Web sites, see the tutorial **Adding a Flash Photo Gallery**, or **Projects: How to add a Flash photo gallery** on the How To tab.

Home Page

About Us

News

Testimonials

Contact Us

Terms of Use

Privacy Policy

Blank Page

Urbanwear

Home

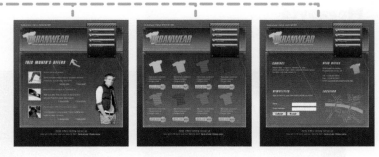

| Offers | Clothing | Contact Us |

+

| Privacy Policy | Terms of Use | Blank Page |

You can use the **Scheme Manager** to choose a new predefined colour scheme for your design template.

Each design offers three colour scheme options specific to that template, but you can also experiment with other predefined colour schemes, or make your own custom scheme.

For more information on colour schemes, see the tutorial **Working With Colour Schemes**.

Megabyte

Contact Us

For information on adding forms to your Web sites, see **Adding forms** in online Help.

Home

New Products

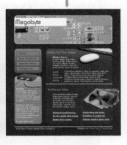

Special Offers

Privacy Policy

Terms of Use

Blank Page

For information on adding e-commerce functionality to your site, see the tutorial **Creating an E-Commerce Web Site**.

Teeb Software

Products

💡 For more information on adding site search functionality, see **Projects: How to add a search facility** on the How To tab.

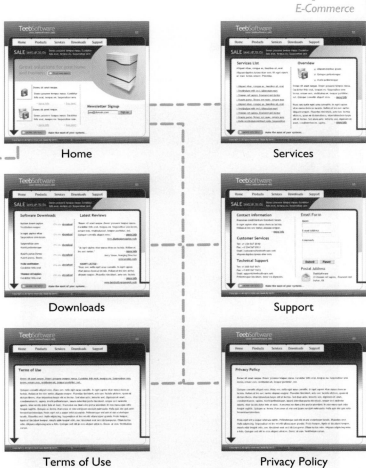

Home

Services

Downloads

Support

Terms of Use

Privacy Policy

Blank Page

The Winery House

Home

For information on adding site search functionality, see **Projects: How to add a search facility** on the How To tab.

About

Wine

Price List

Trips

Contact

Search Results

Privacy Policy

Terms of Use

Blank Page

Natro-Med

Main Page

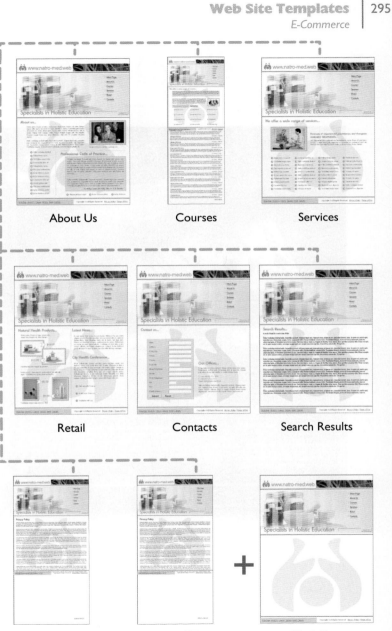

About Us

Courses

Services

Retail

Contacts

Search Results

Privacy Policy

Terms of Use

Blank Page

Casino

Home

Casino   Restaurant   Bar

Games   Contact   Privacy Policy

Terms of Use   +   Blank Page

Fashion E-Mag

Welcome

Beauty & Health

For more information on adding forms to your Web sites, see **Adding forms** in online Help.

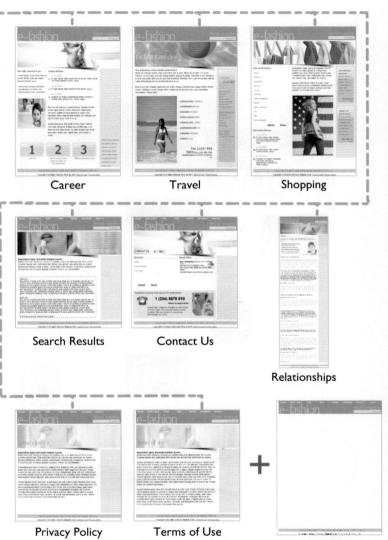

Career

Travel

Shopping

Search Results

Contact Us

Relationships

Privacy Policy

Terms of Use

Blank Page

Our City

Home

For more information on adding calendars to your Web sites, see **Adding content: Adding calendars** on the How To tab.

About

Announcements

Site Seeing

Nightlife

Contact

Search Results

Privacy Policy

Terms of Use

Blank Page

Rock Band Blog

Gallery

For information on adding Flash photo galleries to your Web sites, see the tutorial **Adding a Flash Photo Gallery**, or **Projects: How to add a Flash photo gallery** on the How To tab.

Welcome

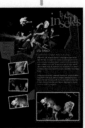

About Us

Contact Us

Privacy Policy

Terms of Use

Blank Page

Sushi Sushi

Reviews

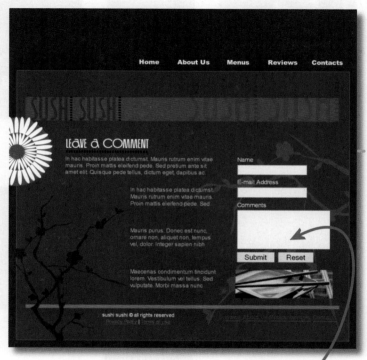

💡 Why not add a comment form for your users to leave a review about your product/service or even the site itself?

For information on adding forms to your Web sites, please see **Adding forms** in online Help.

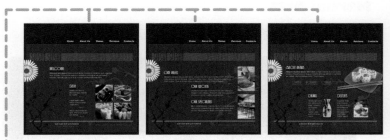

Home   About Us   Menus

Contacts   Privacy Policy   Terms of Use

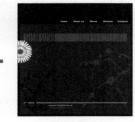

Blank Page

Martial Arts

Classes

> 💡 You can adopt the functionality used in the templates such as these buttons, which take site visitors to another page in your site!
>
> For more information about creating site navigation elements see the tutorial **Building a Web Site**, or **Setting up navigation** on the How To tab.

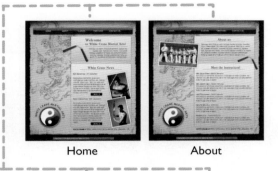

Home   About

Timetable   Contact Us   +

Privacy Policy   Terms of Use   Blank Page

Reactive

Home

welcome

In hac habitasse platea dictumst. Mauris rutrum enim vitae mauris. Proin mattis eleifend pede. Sed pretium ante sit amet elit. Quisque pede tellus, dictum eget, dapibus ac, sodales dictum, lectus. Pellentesque mi dui, molestie sit amet, adipiscing id, iaculis quis, arcu. Nulla tellus sem, viverra eu, ultricies ac, mattis et, velit. Maecenas quis in hac habitasse platea dictumst. Mauris rutrum enim vitae mauris. Proin mattis eleifend pede. Sed pretium ante sit amet elit. Quisque pede tellus, dictum eget, dapibus ac, sodales dictum, lectus. Pellentesque mi dui, molestie sit amet, adipiscing id, iaculis quis, arcu.

Fitness   Bookings   Swimming   Membership

▶ Find your fitness level

Morbi nisl eros, dignissim nec, malesuada et, convallis quis, augue. Vestibulum ante ipsum Morbi nisl eros, dignissim nec, malesuada et, convallis quis, augue. Vestibulum ante.

▶ Centres near you

Morbi nisl eros, dignissim nec, malesuada et, convallis quis, augue. Vestibulum ante ipsum Morbi nisl eros, dignissim nec, malesuada et, convallis quis, augue.

▶ What makes us different

Morbi nisl eros, dignissim nec, malesuada et, convallis quis, augue. Vestibulum ante ipsum Morbi nisl eros, dignissim nec, malesuada et, convallis quis, augue. Vestibulum ante ipsum.

Facilities

Fitness

Bookings

Contact Us

Search Results

Privacy Policy

Terms of Use

Blank Page

Sun Hawk Summer Camp

Home

| Home | Information | Program | Gallery | Leaders | Contacts |

Welcome To Sun Hawk

Quisque pellentesque metus ac quam. Donec magna nulla, aliquet vitae, congue ac, faucibus ut, erat. Donec sit amet neque. Donec posuere tempus massa. Duis vulputate mauris sit amet purus. Duis vestibulum. Fusce ac erat. Curabitur sagittis. Pellentesque ultricies, ante id lobortis feugiat, ipsum magna congue risus, pulvinar euismod arcu nunc ac turpis. Cum sociis natoque penatibus et magnis dis parturient montes, nascetur ridiculus mus.

> Nulla quis nibh. Proin ac pede vel.

> In hac habitasse platea dictumst.

> Amus turpis pede, dignissim sed.

> Nulla vestibulum eleifend nulla.

About Us

Aliquet vitae, congue ac erat.

Pellentesque tincidunt, dolor eu dignissim mollis, justo sapien iaculis pede, vel tincidunt lacus nisl sit amet metus. Fusce ac est vitae purus varius tristique. Phasellus mattis ornare ligula. Donec id nibh. Vestibulum metus quam, ultrices in, sagittis tincidunt, gravida et, sapien. Sed bibendum, lectus vitae tincidunt dapibus, sem felis posuere est.

> Aliquet vitae, congue ac, faucibus ut.

> Vestibulum velit orci, bibendum eget.

> Vivamus vel sapien.

> Mauris purus. Donec est nunc.

Latest Adventure

Curabitur felis erat, tempus eu, placerat et, pellentesque sed, purus. Sed sed diam. Nam nunc. Class aptent taciti sociosqu ad litora torquent per conubia nostra, per inceptos hymenaeos. Aenean risus est. More>>

Home Information Program Gallery Leaders Contacts

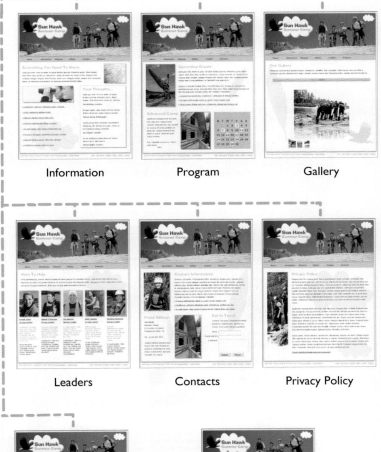

Information

Program

Gallery

Leaders

Contacts

Privacy Policy

Terms of Use

Blank Page

EasyCook

Home

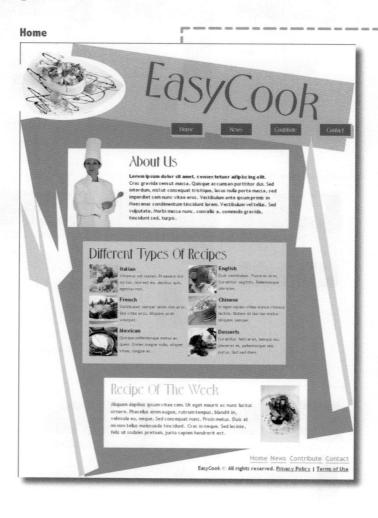

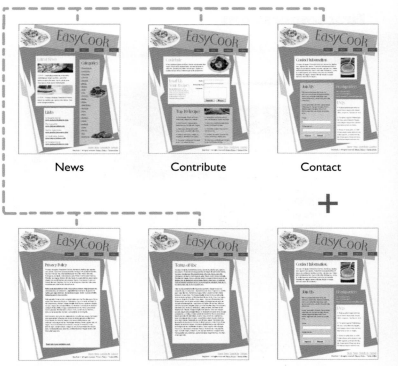

News   Contribute   Contact

Privacy Policy   Terms of Use   Blank Page

You can use the **Scheme Manager** to choose a new predefined colour scheme for your design template.

Each design offers three colour scheme options specific to that template, but you can also experiment with other predefined colour schemes, or make your own custom scheme.

For more information on colour schemes, see the tutorial **Working With Colour Schemes**.

First Impressions

Home

- Home
- About Us
- Get Involved
- Donate
- Contact Us

Welcome...

Maecenas condimentum tincidunt lorem . Vestibulum vel tellus . Sed vulputate. Morbi massa nunc, convallis a, commodo gravida, tincidunt sed, turpis. Aenean ornare viverra est. Maecenas lorem. Aenean euismod iaculis dui. Cum sociis natoque penatibus et magnis dis parturient montes, nascetur ridiculus mus. Nulla quam . Aenean fermentum, turpis sed

What we do

- Aliquam dapibus ipsum vitae
- Sed vulputate
- Aenean ornare viverra est
- Cum sociis natoque penatibus
- Vestibulum vel tellus
- Aenean ornare viverra
- Nulla quam . Aenean
- Maecenas condimentum tincidunt
- Vestibulum vel tellus
- Nulla quam . Aenean fermentum

News

14.05.09
Aliquet non, tempus vel, dolor. Integer sapien nibh, egestas ut, cursus sit amet, faucibus a, sapien. Vestibulum purus purus, elementum ac, luctus ullamcorper, ornare vitae, massa. Nullam posuere sem ut mauris. Nullam velit. Quisque sodales, Donec suscipit suscipit erat. Nam blandit. Praesent congue lorem non dolor. Maecenas vitae erat. Ut ac purus vel purus dapibus gravida.

More info

29.04.09
Nullam lorem sapien, tempus ac, fringilla at, elementum sed, purus. Duis molestie pede. Vivamus quis odio sit amet libero sodales tincidunt. Nam sit amet metus vitae lectus ullamcorper dignissim. Suspendisse leo. Praesent turpis justo, aliquet ac, accumsan vel, posuere quis, pede. Morbi pretium lacus.

More info

We need you...

Aliquam dapibus ipsum vitae sem. Ut eget mauris ac nunc luctus ornare. Phasellus enim augue, rutrum tempus, blandit in, vehicula eu, neque. Sed consequat nunc. Proin metus. Duis at mi non tellus malesuada tincidunt. Cras in neque. Sed lacinia, felis ut sodales pretium, justo sapien hendrerit est, et convallis nisi quam sit amet erat. Suspendisse consequat nibh a mauris. Curabitur libero ligula, faucibus at, mollis ornare, mattis et, libero.

Aliquam pulvinar congue pede. Fusce condimentum turpis vel dolor. Ut blandit. Sed elementum justo quis sem. Sed eu orci eu ante iaculis accumsan. Sed suscipit dolor quis mi. Curabitur ultrices nonummy lacus. Morbi ipsum ipsum, adipiscing eget, tincidunt vitae, pharetra at, tellus. Nulla gravida, arcu eget dictum elet, velit ligula suscipit nibh, sagittis imperdiet metus nunc non pede. Aenean congue pede in nisl tristique interdum. Sed commodo, ipsum ac dignissim ullamcorper, odio nulla venenatis

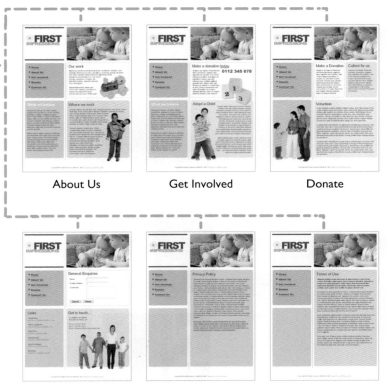

About Us

Get Involved

Donate

Contact Us

Privacy Policy

Terms of Use

+

Blank Page

Green Park

Home

About the Park

Curabitur felis erat, tempus eu, placerat et, pellentesque sed, purus. Sed sed diam. Nam nunc. Class aptent taciti sociosqu ad litora torquent per conubia nostra, per.
More

The History

Nulla quis nibh. Proin ac pede vel ligula facilisis gravida. Phasellus purus. Etiam sapien. Duis diam urna, iaculis ut, vehicula ac, varius sit amet, mi. Donec id nisl. Aliquam erat volutpat. Integer fringilla. Duis lobortis, quam non volutpat.
More

Visit our Farmyard

Nulla quis nibh. Proin ac pede vel ligula facilisis gravida. Phasellus purus. Etiam sapien. Duis diam urna, iaculis ut, vehicula ac, varius sit amet, mi. Donec id nisl. Aliquam erat volutpat. Integer fringilla. Duis lobortis, quam non volutpat.
More

Welcome to Green Park!

Curabitur felis erat, tempus eu, placerat et, pellentesque sed, purus. Sed sed diam. Nam nunc. Class aptent taciti sociosqu ad litora torquent per conubia nostra, per. Curabitur felis erat, tempus eu, placerat et, pellentesque sed, purus. Sed sed diam. Nam nunc. Class aptent taciti sociosqu ad litora torquent per conubia nostra, per. Curabitur felis erat, tempus eu, placerat et, pellentesque sed, purus. Sed sed diam. Nam nunc. Class aptent taciti sociosqu ad litora torquent.

Morbi pellentesque mauris interdum porta

Should the park be open until 8pm?

Opinions?

Opinions?
- Strongly agree
- Agree
- Neither
- Disagree
- Strongly disagree

[Vote]

News

Vivamus vel sapien. Praesent nisl tortor, laoreel eu, dapibus quis, egestas non, mauris. Cum sociis natoque penatibus et magnis dis parturient montes, nascetur ridiculus mus. Nullam eleifend pharetra felis. Mauris nibh velit, tristique ac, lacinia in, scelerisque at, ante. Donec viverra tortor sed nulla.

Morbi nisl eros, dignissim nec, malesuada et, convallis quis, augue. Vestibulum ante ipsum primis in faucibus orci luctus et ultrices posuere cubilia Curae. Proin aliquam, leo at luctus tempus, eros lectus eleifend massa, quis sollicitudin erat magna non leo. Vestibulum vel metus. Donec sagittis velit vel augue. Fusce in nisl vitae massa venenatis rhoncus. Praesent orci velit, lobortis eget, suscipit semper, congue eu, est. Quisque malesuada volutpat enim. Vestibulum leo sem, molestie a, mattis bibendum, feugiat facilisis, nisl. Nam scelerisque odio. Suspendisse fermentum faucibus felis. Praesent pharetra, in consequat felis in tellus. In mi enim, rhoncus ullamcorper, sagittis at, placerat eget, mauris. Suspendisse auctor erat at ipsum. Aliquam vitae tortor id massa tincidunt eleifend.

In hac habitasse platea dictumst. Mauris rutrum eros vitae mauris. Proin mattis eleifend pede. Sed pretium ante sit amet elit. Quisque pede tellus, dictum eget, dapibus ac, sodales dictum, lectus. Pellentesque mi dui, molestie sit amet, adipiscing id, iaculis quis, arcu. Nulla tellus sem, viverra eu, ultricies ac, mattis et, velit. Maecenas quis magna. Ut viverra nisl eu ipsum. Maecenas rhoncus. Duis mattis nisi nec sapien. Nullam eu ante non enim tincidunt fringilla. Integer leo. Duis eget enim.

Curabitur felis erat, tempus eu, placerat et, pellentesque sed, purus. Sed sed diam. Nam nunc. Class aptent taciti sociosqu ad litora torquent per conubia nostra, per inceptos hymenaeos. Aenean risus est, porttitor vel, placerat at amet, vestibulum sit amet, nibh. Ut faucibus justo quis nisl. Etiam vulputate, sapien eu egestas rutrum, leo neque luctus dolor, sed hendrerit tortor metus ut dui.

Newsletter Signup

Suspendisse ligula. Sed mollis tristique mauris. Nullam nunc nunc, aliquet et, tristique nec, porttitor quis, urna. Etiam eu erat. Morbi id nisl. Curabitur semper sem. Nulla turpis nibh, tempor nec, aliquet vitae, elementum ac, mauris.

you@domain.com [Sign up]

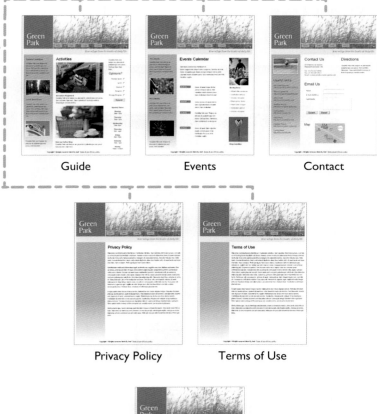

Guide

Events

Contact

Privacy Policy

Terms of Use

Blank Page

Street Level

Welcome

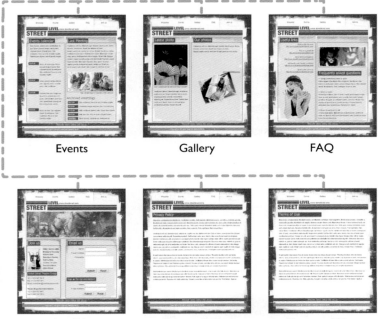

Events

Gallery

FAQ

Join Us

Privacy Policy

Terms of Use

💡 You can adopt the functionality used in the templates such as Flash photo galleries, (see the 'Gallery' page in this site).

For information on adding Flash photo galleries to your Web sites, see the tutorial **Adding a Flash Photo Gallery**, or **Adding content: Working with images** on the How To tab.

+

Blank Page

Amelia

Home

Amelia

Our New Born Baby

126 days old!

Home About Me Photos Diary Guest Book

Welcome!

met justo. In velit. Vivamus turpis pede, dignissim sed, scelerisque nec, pretium sit amet, dui. Nam nec felis non turpis hendrerit varius. In ultrices ornare lorem. Quisque bibendum, massa sed venenatis malesuada, diam ipsum blandit urna, vel ultricies pede nulla vitae lacus.

Lorem ipsum dolor sit amet, consectetuer adipiscing elit. Quisque in augue. Donec aliquam magna nonummy enim. Proin blandit imperdiet sem. Donec malesuada, urna sit amet varius

Social Events

May 27th - Christening at Ellen's Church
gravida. Phasellus purus. Etiam sapien. Duis diam urna, iaculis ut, vehicula ac, varius sit amet, mi. Donec id nisl. Aliquam erat volutpat. Integer fringilla. Duis lobortis, quam non volutpat suscipit, magna sem consequat libero, ac hendrerit urna ante id mi. Quisque commodo facilisis tellus. Integer sodales lorem sed nisl. Morbi consectetuer mauris quis odio. Ut dolor lorem, viverra vitae, viverra eu, euismod nec, enim. Lorem ipsum dolor sit amet, consectetuer adipiscing elit.

August 2nd - Amelia's First Holiday
Morbi nisl eros, dignissim nec, malesuada et, convallis quis, augue. Vestibulum ante ipsum primis in faucibus orci luctus et ultrices posuere cubilia Curae; Proin aliquam, leo at luctus tempus, eros lectus eleifend massa, quis sollicitudin erat magna non leo. Vestibulum vel metus. Donec sagittis velit vel augue. Fusce in nisl vitae massa venenatis rhoncus. Praesent orci velit, lobortis eget, suscipit semper, congue eu, est. Quisque malesuada volutpat enim. Vestibulum leo sem, molestie a, mattis bibendum, feugiat facilisis, nisl. Nam scelerisque odio. Suspendisse fermentum faucibus felis.

Praesent orci velit, lobortis eget, suscipit semper, congue eu, est. Quisque malesuada volutpat enim. Vestibulum leo sem, molestie a, mattis bibendum, feugiat facilisis, nisl. Nam scelerisque odio. Suspendisse fermentum faucibus felis.

About Me

Photos

Diary

Guest Book

Privacy Policy

Terms of Use

Blank Page

Ceramic Artist

Gallery

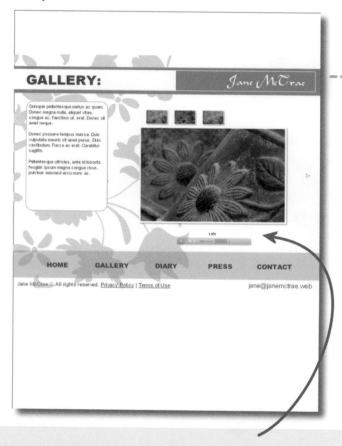

For information on adding Flash photo galleries to your Web sites, see the tutorial **Adding a Flash Photo Gallery**, or **Projects: How to add a Flash photo gallery** on the How To tab.

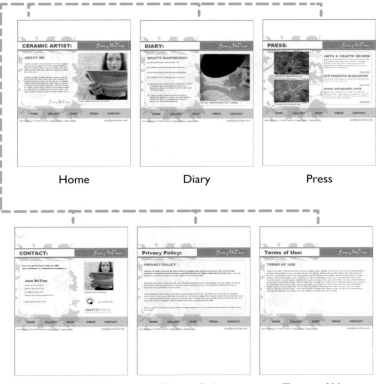

Home

Diary

Press

Contact

Privacy Policy

Terms of Use

Blank Page

Holiday Blog

About

Gallery

Contact

Privacy Policy

Terms of Use

Blank Page

Our Baby Boy

Home

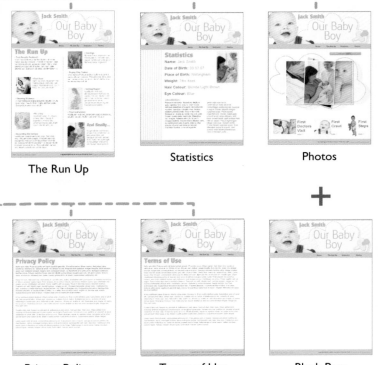

The Run Up

Statistics

Photos

+

Privacy Policy

Terms of Use

Blank Page

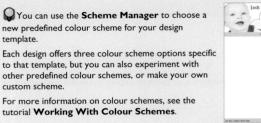

You can use the **Scheme Manager** to choose a new predefined colour scheme for your design template.

Each design offers three colour scheme options specific to that template, but you can also experiment with other predefined colour schemes, or make your own custom scheme.

For more information on colour schemes, see the tutorial **Working With Colour Schemes**.

Special Day

Home

About Us

Services

Sale

Contact

Terms of Use

Privacy Policy

Blank Page

T.Reinn

Home

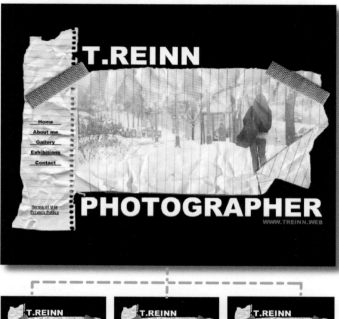

Contact

Privacy Policy

Privacy Policy

+

Blank Page

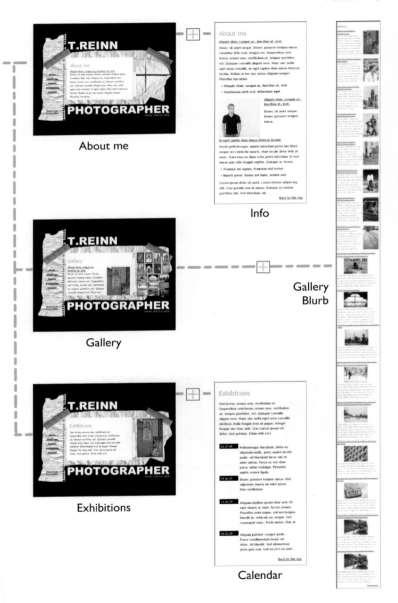

About me

Info

Gallery

Gallery Blurb

Exhibitions

Calendar

Reactive

Teeb Software

The Winery House

Holiday Blog

Our Holiday

Birthday Invite

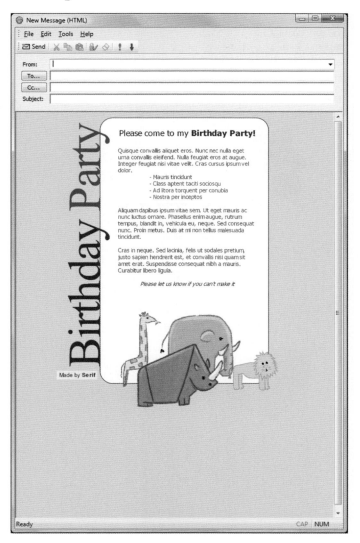

It's a Boy

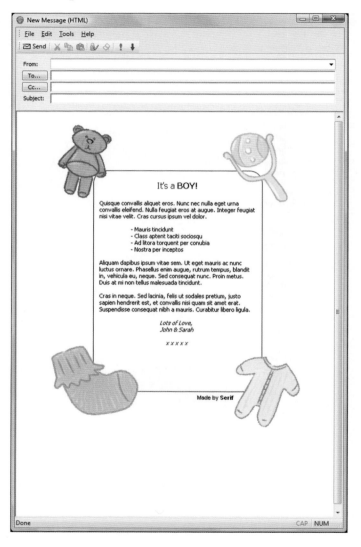

Our Baby

Picture Frames

Rock Band Blog

Theme Graphics

Theme Graphics

WebPlus X2 includes a wide range of theme graphics—pre-designed elements that you can add to your site with a single click. Theme graphics range from static design elements, like bullets and headings, to navigation elements such as navigation bars, and Previous and Next buttons—all pre-programmed to adapt to the site structure you've defined. Once you've added a theme graphic to your page, you can edit its properties (text, fill colour, and so on) and can also instantly update any or all elements by selecting a different theme.

For more information on using Theme Graphics in your site, please see the tutorial **Using Theme Graphics and the Gallery**.

WebPlus theme graphics have their own colour scheme, which you can easily modify yourself. Alternatively, use the **Scheme Manager** to apply a different pre-defined WebPlus colour scheme to your theme graphics!

Ahead

Navbars

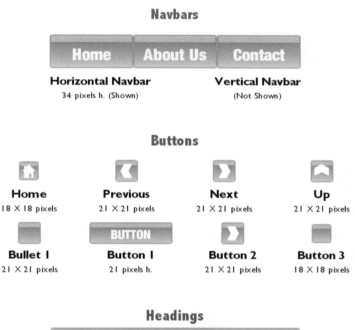

Horizontal Navbar
34 pixels h. (Shown)

Vertical Navbar
(Not Shown)

Buttons

Home
18 × 18 pixels

Previous
21 × 21 pixels

Next
21 × 21 pixels

Up
21 × 21 pixels

Bullet 1
21 × 21 pixels

Button 1
21 pixels h.

Button 2
21 × 21 pixels

Button 3
18 × 18 pixels

Headings

HEADING TEXT
250 × 34 pixels

Heading 2: 350 × 34 pixels
Heading 3: 350 × 34 pixels
Heading 4: 350 × 34 pixels

Horizontal Strip 750 × 34 pixels

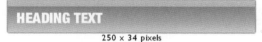

Beacon

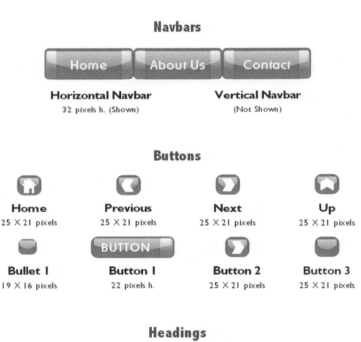

Navbars

Horizontal Navbar
32 pixels h. (Shown)

Vertical Navbar
(Not Shown)

Buttons

Home
25 × 21 pixels

Previous
25 × 21 pixels

Next
25 × 21 pixels

Up
25 × 21 pixels

Bullet 1
19 × 16 pixels

Button 1
22 pixels h.

Button 2
25 × 21 pixels

Button 3
25 × 21 pixels

Headings

250 × 22 pixels
Heading 2: 350 × 22 pixels
Heading 3: 500 × 22 pixels
Heading 4: 750 × 22 pixels

Horizontal Strip 750 × 41 pixels

Bold

Navbars

Home   **About Us**   **Contact**

Horizontal Navbar   **Vertical Navbar**

32 pixels h. (Shown)   (Not Shown)

Buttons

Home

19 × 21 pixels

Previous

22 × 22 pixels

Next

22 × 22 pixels

Up

22 × 22 pixels

Bullet 1

21 × 21 pixels

BUTTON

Button 1

32 pixels h.

Button 2

22 × 22 pixels

Button 3

19 × 19 pixels

Headings

HEADING TEXT

250 × 32 pixels

Heading 2: 350 × 32 pixels
Heading 3: 500 × 32 pixels
Heading 4: 750 × 32 pixels

Horizontal Strip 750 × 34 pixels

Bright

Navbars

Horizontal Navbar
35 pixels h. (Shown)

Vertical Navbar
(Not Shown)

Buttons

Home
26 × 26 pixels

Previous
26 × 26 pixels

Next
26 × 26 pixels

Up
26 × 26 pixels

Bullet I
16 × 15 pixels

Button I
26 pixels h.

Button 2
26 × 26 pixels

Button 3
26 × 26 pixels

Headings

HEADING TEXT

250 × 27 pixels
Heading 2: 350 × 27 pixels
Heading 3: 500 × 27 pixels
Heading 4: 750 × 27 pixels

Horizontal Strip 750 × 36 pixels

Candy

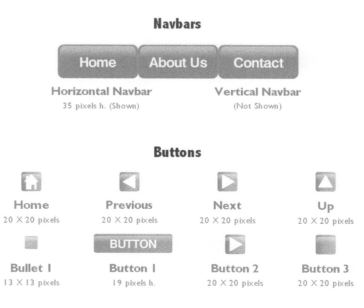

Navbars

Horizontal Navbar
35 pixels h. (Shown)

Vertical Navbar
(Not Shown)

Buttons

Home
20 × 20 pixels

Previous
20 × 20 pixels

Next
20 × 20 pixels

Up
20 × 20 pixels

Bullet 1
13 × 13 pixels

Button 1
19 pixels h.

Button 2
20 × 20 pixels

Button 3
20 × 20 pixels

Headings

HEADING TEXT

250 × 27 pixels
Heading 2: 350 × 27 pixels
Heading 3: 500 × 27 pixels
Heading 4: 750 × 27 pixels

Horizontal Strip 750 × 31 pixels

Clean

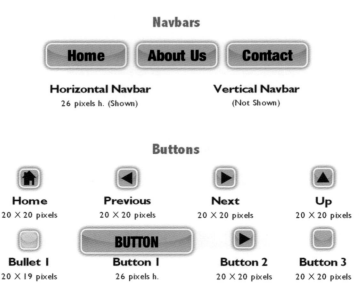

Navbars

Home   **About Us**   **Contact**

Horizontal Navbar
26 pixels h. (Shown)

Vertical Navbar
(Not Shown)

Buttons

Home
20 × 20 pixels

Previous
20 × 20 pixels

Next
20 × 20 pixels

Up
20 × 20 pixels

Bullet I
20 × 19 pixels

BUTTON

Button I
26 pixels h.

Button 2
20 × 20 pixels

Button 3
20 × 20 pixels

Headings

HEADING TEXT

250 × 26 pixels
Heading 2: 350 × 26 pixels
Heading 3: 500 × 26 pixels
Heading 4: 750 × 26 pixels

Horizontal Strip 750 × 35 pixels

Computer

Navbars

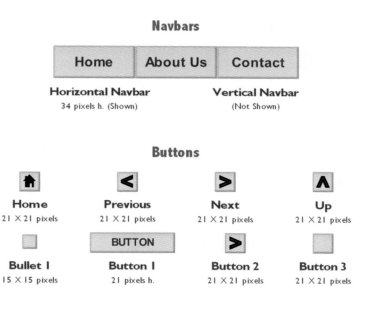

Horizontal Navbar
34 pixels h. (Shown)

Vertical Navbar
(Not Shown)

Buttons

Home
21 × 21 pixels

Previous
21 × 21 pixels

Next
21 × 21 pixels

Up
21 × 21 pixels

Bullet 1
15 × 15 pixels

Button 1
21 pixels h.

Button 2
21 × 21 pixels

Button 3
21 × 21 pixels

Headings

HEADING TEXT

250 × 23 pixels
Heading 2: 350 × 23 pixels
Heading 3: 500 × 23 pixels
Heading 4: 750 × 23 pixels

Horizontal Strip 750 × 34 pixels

Dream

Navbars

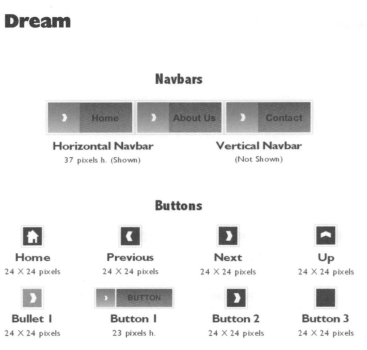

Horizontal Navbar
37 pixels h. (Shown)

Vertical Navbar
(Not Shown)

Buttons

Home
24 × 24 pixels

Previous
24 × 24 pixels

Next
24 × 24 pixels

Up
24 × 24 pixels

Bullet 1
24 × 24 pixels

Button 1
23 pixels h.

Button 2
24 × 24 pixels

Button 3
24 × 24 pixels

Headings

250 × 28 pixels
Heading 2: 350 × 28 pixels
Heading 3: 500 × 28 pixels
Heading 4: 750 × 28 pixels

Horizontal Strip 750 × 35 pixels

Drop

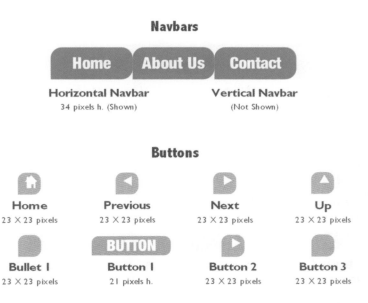

Navbars

Horizontal Navbar
34 pixels h. (Shown)

Vertical Navbar
(Not Shown)

Buttons

Home
23 × 23 pixels

Previous
23 × 23 pixels

Next
23 × 23 pixels

Up
23 × 23 pixels

Bullet 1
23 × 23 pixels

Button 1
21 pixels h.

Button 2
23 × 23 pixels

Button 3
23 × 23 pixels

Headings

250 × 25 pixels
Heading 2: 350 × 25 pixels
Heading 3: 500 × 25 pixels
Heading 4: 750 × 25 pixels

Horizontal Strip 750 × 34 pixels

Gel

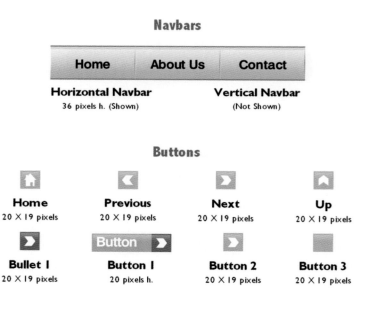

Navbars

Horizontal Navbar
36 pixels h. (Shown)

Vertical Navbar
(Not Shown)

Buttons

Home
20 × 19 pixels

Previous
20 × 19 pixels

Next
20 × 19 pixels

Up
20 × 19 pixels

Bullet 1
20 × 19 pixels

Button 1
20 pixels h.

Button 2
20 × 19 pixels

Button 3
20 × 19 pixels

Headings

HEADING TEXT

250 × 27 pixels
Heading 2: 350 × 27 pixels
Heading 3: 500 × 27 pixels
Heading 4: 750 × 27 pixels

Horizontal Strip 750 × 36 pixels

Glass

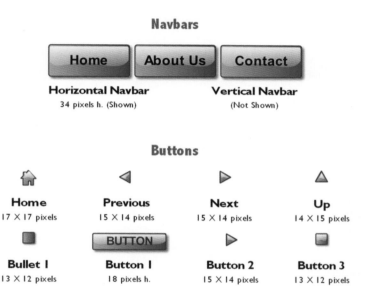

Navbars

Home   **About Us**   **Contact**

Horizontal Navbar   **Vertical Navbar**

34 pixels h. (Shown)   (Not Shown)

Buttons

Home   **Previous**   **Next**   **Up**

17 × 17 pixels   15 × 14 pixels   15 × 14 pixels   14 × 15 pixels

Bullet 1   **Button 1**   **Button 2**   **Button 3**

13 × 12 pixels   18 pixels h.   15 × 14 pixels   13 × 12 pixels

Headings

HEADING TEXT

250 × 30 pixels

Heading 2: 350 × 30 pixels

Heading 3: 500 × 30 pixels

Heading 4: 750 × 30 pixels

Horizontal Strip 750 × 24 pixels

Ice

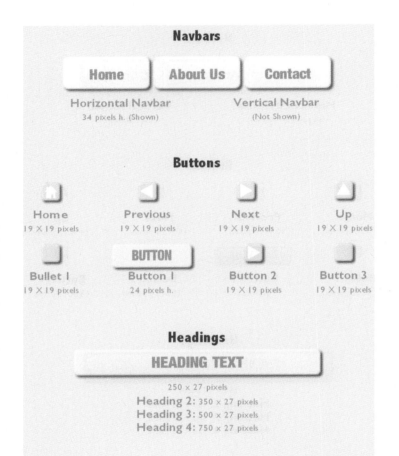

Navbars

Home   About Us   Contact

Horizontal Navbar
34 pixels h. (Shown)

Vertical Navbar
(Not Shown)

Buttons

Home
19 × 19 pixels

Previous
19 × 19 pixels

Next
19 × 19 pixels

Up
19 × 19 pixels

Bullet 1
19 × 19 pixels

BUTTON
Button 1
24 pixels h.

Button 2
19 × 19 pixels

Button 3
19 × 19 pixels

Headings

HEADING TEXT

250 × 27 pixels
Heading 2: 350 × 27 pixels
Heading 3: 500 × 27 pixels
Heading 4: 750 × 27 pixels

Horizontal Strip 750 × 34 pixels

Market

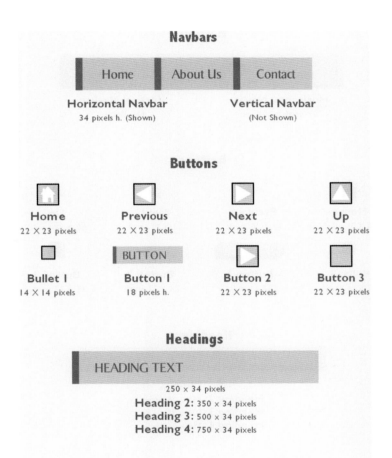

Navbars

Home | About Us | Contact

Horizontal Navbar
34 pixels h. (Shown)

Vertical Navbar
(Not Shown)

Buttons

Home
22 X 23 pixels

Previous
22 X 23 pixels

Next
22 X 23 pixels

Up
22 X 23 pixels

Bullet 1
14 X 14 pixels

BUTTON
Button 1
18 pixels h.

Button 2
22 X 23 pixels

Button 3
22 X 23 pixels

Headings

HEADING TEXT

250 x 34 pixels
Heading 2: 350 x 34 pixels
Heading 3: 500 x 34 pixels
Heading 4: 750 x 34 pixels

Horizontal Strip 750 x 34 pixels

Metal

Navbars

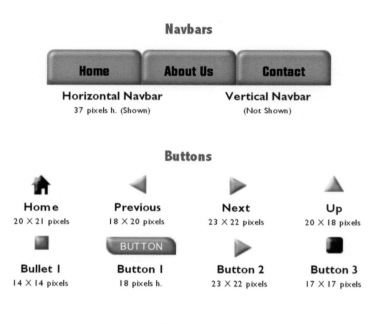

Horizontal Navbar
37 pixels h. (Shown)

Vertical Navbar
(Not Shown)

Buttons

Home
20 X 21 pixels

Previous
18 X 20 pixels

Next
23 X 22 pixels

Up
20 X 18 pixels

Bullet I
14 X 14 pixels

Button I
18 pixels h.

Button 2
23 X 22 pixels

Button 3
17 X 17 pixels

Headings

NAVBAR TEXT

250 × 25 pixels
Heading 2: 350 × 25 pixels
Heading 3: 500 × 25 pixels
Heading 4: 750 × 25 pixels

Horizontal Strip 750 × 37 pixels

Metro

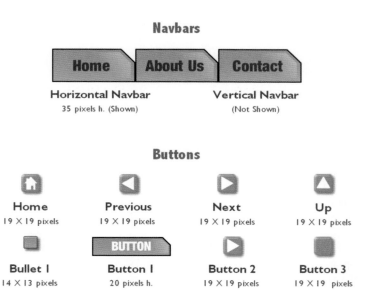

Navbars

Horizontal Navbar
35 pixels h. (Shown)

Vertical Navbar
(Not Shown)

Buttons

Home
19 X 19 pixels

Previous
19 X 19 pixels

Next
19 X 19 pixels

Up
19 X 19 pixels

Bullet 1
14 X 13 pixels

Button 1
20 pixels h.

Button 2
19 X 19 pixels

Button 3
19 X 19 pixels

Headings

250 × 23 pixels
Heading 2: 350 × 23 pixels
Heading 3: 500 × 23 pixels
Heading 4: 750 × 23 pixels

Horizontal Strip 750 × 36 pixels

Micro

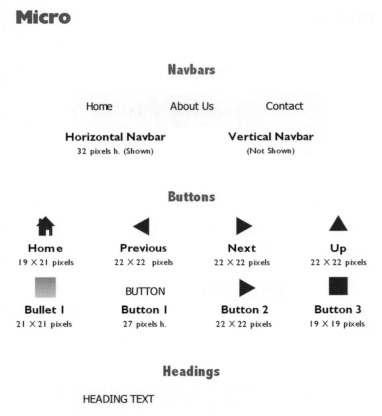

Navbars

Home   About Us   Contact

Horizontal Navbar   **Vertical Navbar**
32 pixels h. (Shown)   (Not Shown)

Buttons

Home
19 X 21 pixels

Previous
22 X 22 pixels

Next
22 X 22 pixels

Up
22 X 22 pixels

Bullet 1
21 X 21 pixels

BUTTON
Button 1
27 pixels h.

Button 2
22 X 22 pixels

Button 3
19 X 19 pixels

Headings

HEADING TEXT

250 × 32 pixels
Heading 2: 350 × 32 pixels
Heading 3: 500 × 32 pixels
Heading 4: 750 × 32 pixels

Horizontal Strip 750 × 34 pixels

Plastic

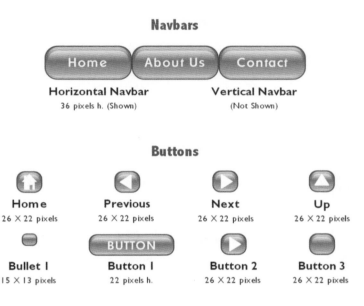

Navbars

Horizontal Navbar
36 pixels h. (Shown)

Vertical Navbar
(Not Shown)

Buttons

Home
26 × 22 pixels

Previous
26 × 22 pixels

Next
26 × 22 pixels

Up
26 × 22 pixels

Bullet 1
15 × 13 pixels

Button 1
22 pixels h.

Button 2
26 × 22 pixels

Button 3
26 × 22 pixels

Headings

250 × 22 pixels
Heading 2: 350 × 22 pixels
Heading 3: 500 × 22 pixels
Heading 4: 750 × 22 pixels

Horizontal Strip 750 × 32 pixels

React

Navbars

Home   **About Us**   **Contact**

Horizontal Navbar   **Vertical Navbar**
34 pixels h. (Shown)   (Not Shown)

Buttons

Home   **Previous**   **Next**   **Up**
23 × 23 pixels   23 × 23 pixels   23 × 23 pixels   23 × 23 pixels

Bullet I   **Button I**   **Button 2**   **Button 3**
14 × 9 pixels   19 pixels h.   23 × 23 pixels   23 × 23 pixels

BUTTON

Headings

 HEADING TEXT

250 × 34 pixels
Heading 2: 350 × 34 pixels
Heading 3: 500 × 34 pixels
Heading 4: 750 × 34 pixels

Horizontal Strip 750 × 34 pixels

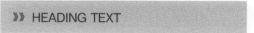

Reflect

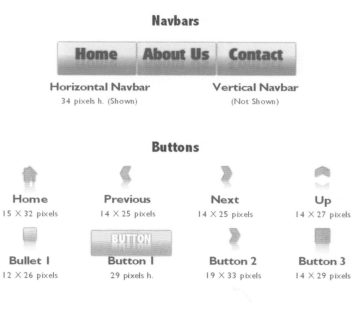

Navbars

Horizontal Navbar
34 pixels h. (Shown)

Vertical Navbar
(Not Shown)

Buttons

Home
15 × 32 pixels

Previous
14 × 25 pixels

Next
14 × 25 pixels

Up
14 × 27 pixels

Bullet 1
12 × 26 pixels

Button 1
29 pixels h.

Button 2
19 × 33 pixels

Button 3
14 × 29 pixels

Headings

250 × 34 pixels
Heading 2: 350 × 34 pixels
Heading 3: 500 × 34 pixels
Heading 4: 750 × 34 pixels

Horizontal Strip 750 × 34 pixels

Rounded

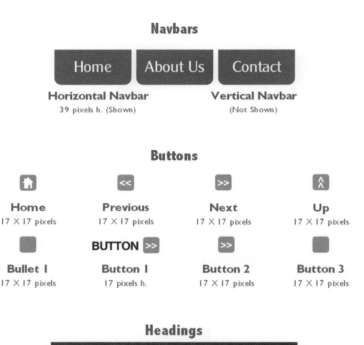

Navbars

Home   About Us   Contact

Horizontal Navbar
39 pixels h. (Shown)

Vertical Navbar
(Not Shown)

Buttons

Home
17 × 17 pixels

Previous
17 × 17 pixels

Next
17 × 17 pixels

Up
17 × 17 pixels

Bullet 1
17 × 17 pixels

Button 1
17 pixels h.

Button 2
17 × 17 pixels

Button 3
17 × 17 pixels

Headings

HEADING TEXT

250 × 25 pixels
Heading 2: 350 × 25 pixels
Heading 3: 500 × 25 pixels
Heading 4: 750 × 25 pixels

Horizontal Strip 750 × 27 pixels

Silver

Navbars

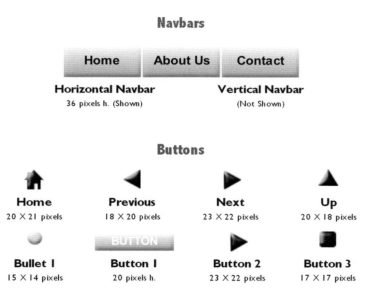

Horizontal Navbar

36 pixels h. (Shown)

Vertical Navbar

(Not Shown)

Buttons

Home

20 × 21 pixels

Previous

18 × 20 pixels

Next

23 × 22 pixels

Up

20 × 18 pixels

Bullet I

15 × 14 pixels

Button I

20 pixels h.

Button 2

23 × 22 pixels

Button 3

17 × 17 pixels

Headings

HEADING TEXT

250 × 27 pixels

Heading 2: 350 × 27 pixels
Heading 3: 500 × 27 pixels
Heading 4: 750 × 27 pixels

Horizontal Strip 750 × 36 pixels

Simple

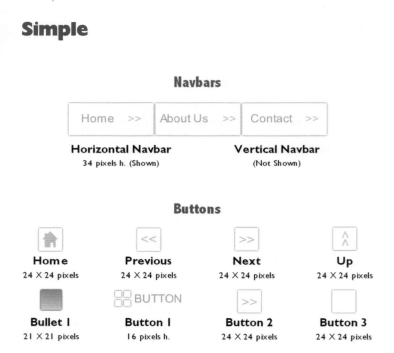

Navbars

Horizontal Navbar
34 pixels h. (Shown)

Vertical Navbar
(Not Shown)

Buttons

Home
24 × 24 pixels

Previous
24 × 24 pixels

Next
24 × 24 pixels

Up
24 × 24 pixels

Bullet 1
21 × 21 pixels

Button 1
16 pixels h.

Button 2
24 × 24 pixels

Button 3
24 × 24 pixels

Headings

HEADING TEXT

250 × 34 pixels
Heading 2: 350 × 34 pixels
Heading 3: 500 × 34 pixels
Heading 4: 750 × 34 pixels

Horizontal Strip 750 × 34 pixels

Sky

Navbars

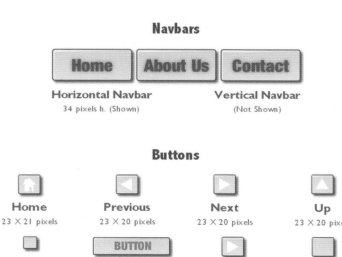

Horizontal Navbar
34 pixels h. (Shown)

Vertical Navbar
(Not Shown)

Buttons

Home
23 × 21 pixels

Previous
23 × 20 pixels

Next
23 × 20 pixels

Up
23 × 20 pixels

Bullet 1
14 × 13 pixels

Button 1
19 pixels h.

Button 2
23 × 20 pixels

Button 3
23 × 21 pixels

Headings

250 × 23 pixels
Heading 2: 350 × 23 pixels
Heading 3: 500 × 23 pixels
Heading 4: 750 × 23 pixels

Horizontal Strip 750 × 34 pixels

Soft

Navbars

Horizontal Navbar
37 pixels h. (Shown)

Vertical Navbar
(Not Shown)

Buttons

Home
19 × 19 pixels

Previous
19 × 19 pixels

Next
19 × 19 pixels

Up
19 × 19 pixels

Bullet 1
18 × 17 pixels

Button 1
20 pixels h.

Button 2
19 × 19 pixels

Button 3
19 × 19 pixels

Headings

HEADING TEXT

250 × 24 pixels
Heading 2: 350 × 24 pixels
Heading 3: 500 × 24 pixels
Heading 4: 750 × 24 pixels

Horizontal Strip 750 × 27 pixels

Spirit

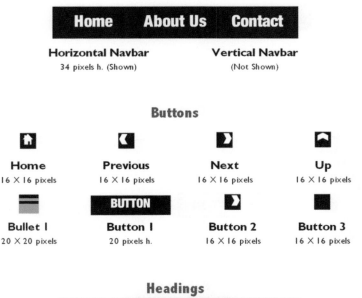

Navbars

Horizontal Navbar
34 pixels h. (Shown)

Vertical Navbar
(Not Shown)

Buttons

Home
16 X 16 pixels

Previous
16 X 16 pixels

Next
16 X 16 pixels

Up
16 X 16 pixels

Bullet 1
20 X 20 pixels

Button 1
20 pixels h.

Button 2
16 X 16 pixels

Button 3
16 X 16 pixels

Headings

250 × 27 pixels
Heading 2: 350 × 27 pixels
Heading 3: 500 × 27 pixels
Heading 4: 750 × 27 pixels

Horizontal Strip 750 × 34 pixels

Tab

Navbars

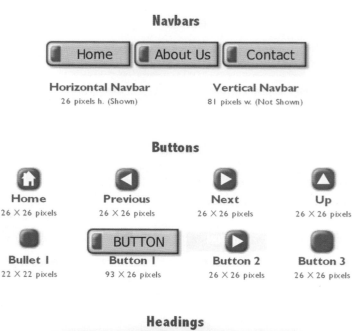

Horizontal Navbar
26 pixels h. (Shown)

Vertical Navbar
81 pixels w. (Not Shown)

Buttons

Home
26 × 26 pixels

Previous
26 × 26 pixels

Next
26 × 26 pixels

Up
26 × 26 pixels

Bullet 1
22 × 22 pixels

Button 1
93 × 26 pixels

Button 2
26 × 26 pixels

Button 3
26 × 26 pixels

Headings

HEADING TEXT

250 × 26 pixels
Heading 2: 350 × 26 pixels
Heading 3: 500 × 26 pixels
Heading 4: 750 × 26 pixels

Horizontal Strip 750 × 37 pixels

Tall

Navbars

Horizontal Navbar
32 pixels h. (Shown)

Vertical Navbar
(Not Shown)

Buttons

Home
19 × 21 pixels

Previous
22 × 22 pixels

Next
22 × 22 pixels

Up
22 × 22 pixels

Bullet 1
21 × 21 pixels

Button 1
32 pixels h.

Button 2
22 × 22 pixels

Button 3
19 × 19 pixels

Headings

HEADING TEXT

250 × 32 pixels
Heading 2: 350 × 32 pixels
Heading 3: 500 × 32 pixels
Heading 4: 750 × 32 pixels

Horizontal Strip 750 × 34 pixels

Traditional

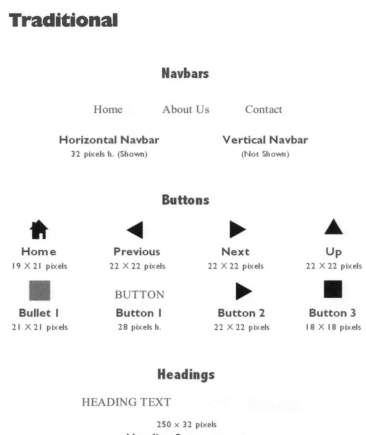

Navbars

Home   About Us   Contact

Horizontal Navbar
32 pixels h. (Shown)

Vertical Navbar
(Not Shown)

Buttons

Home
19 × 21 pixels

Previous
22 × 22 pixels

Next
22 × 22 pixels

Up
22 × 22 pixels

Bullet 1
21 × 21 pixels

BUTTON
Button 1
28 pixels h.

Button 2
22 × 22 pixels

Button 3
18 × 18 pixels

Headings

HEADING TEXT

250 × 32 pixels
Heading 2: 350 × 32 pixels
Heading 3: 500 × 32 pixels
Heading 4: 750 × 32 pixels

Horizontal Strip 750 × 34 pixels

Werk

Navbars

| Home | About Us | Contact |

Horizontal Navbar
27 pixels h. (Shown)

Vertical Navbar
(Not Shown)

Buttons

Home
19 × 19 pixels

Previous
19 × 19 pixels

Next
19 × 19 pixels

Up
19 × 19 pixels

Bullet 1
19 × 19 pixels

Button 1
21 pixels h.

Button 2
19 × 19 pixels

Button 3
19 × 19 pixels

Headings

HEADING TEXT

250 × 28 pixels
Heading 2: 350 × 28 pixels
Heading 3: 500 × 28 pixels
Heading 4: 750 × 28 pixels

Horizontal Strip 750 × 35 pixels

Zeal

Navbars

Horizontal Navbar
38 pixels h. (Shown)

Vertical Navbar
(Not Shown)

Buttons

Home
28 × 26 pixels

Previous
28 × 26 pixels

Next
28 × 26 pixels

Up
28 × 26 pixels

Bullet 1
13 × 13 pixels

Button 1
18 pixels h.

Button 2
28 × 26 pixels

Button 3
28 × 26 pixels

Headings

HEADING TEXT

250 × 29 pixels
Heading 2: 350 × 29 pixels
Heading 3: 500 × 29 pixels
Heading 4: 750 × 29 pixels

Horizontal Strip 750 × 33 pixels

Colour Schemes

Colour Schemes

WebPlus X2 provides you with a selection of colour schemes, which you can apply to your own site or use to update a design template site.

Using Colour Schemes

In WebPlus, a colour scheme is a basic group of five colours, with additional colours for hyperlink and rollover text (**H**yperlink, **F**ollowed Hyperlink, **A**ctive Hyperlink, **R**ollover) and for **B**ackground and **O**n-page colour. Colour schemes work like a paint-by-numbers system, where various regions of a layout are coded with numbers, and a specific colour is assigned to each region. The Scheme Manager displays a selection of preset schemes, which you can select and apply at any time during the design process.

The WebPlus design templates are excellent examples of Web sites designed with colour schemes—open a template, then in the Scheme Manager, click to select a different colour scheme for that template. Elements in the design will change colour to match the chosen scheme. You can switch to a different colour scheme when you first open a template from the Startup wizard.

Atlantis

Chocolate

Fields

Lizard

Marina

Melons

Military

Monotone

Mushroom

Nursery

Orange Tree

Pinks

Plants

Red

Roses

Safari

Stones

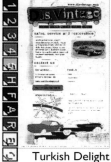

Turkish Delight